Recipe for a Country Inn

ALSO BY DONNA LEAHY

Morning Glories

Recipe for a Country Inn

Fine Food from the Inn at Twin Linden

DONNA LEAHY

WM

WILLIAM MORROW

An Imprint of HarperCollinsPublishers

HarperCollins books may be purchased for educational, business, or sales promotional use. For information please write: Special Markets Department, HarperCollins Publishers Inc., 10 East 53rd Street, New York, NY 10022.

FIRST EDITION

Photographs by Bob Leahy
Food photographs by Ellen Silverman
Food styling by Anne Disrude
Prop styling by Betty Alfenito

Printed on acid-free paper

Library of Congress Cataloging-in-Publication Data

Leahy, Donna.
    Recipe for a country inn : fine food from the Inn at Twin Linden /
Donna Leahy.— 1st ed.
        p.   cm.
    Includes index.
    ISBN 0-06-018492-2
    1. Cookery, American.   2. Inn at Twin Linden
(Churchtown, Pa.)   I. Title.

    TX715 .L4153   2002
    641.5'09748'15—dc21

                                                    2001026693

02   03   04   05   06   IM   10   9   8   7   6   5   4   3   2   1

For my partner, my love, my favorite photographer
and my best friend, Bob

And for my best dog and second best overall friend—
we miss you Mr. Smokey

CONTENTS

ACKNOWLEDGMENTS

We have entertained so many angels unaware through the years. We are grateful to each and every one of our wonderful guests for choosing to stay with us. We have also had the pleasure to work with so many great people at the Inn. Thank you to all of our staff throughout the years.

Dan Green—besides being our terrific agent, you and Jane are among our most enjoyable guests.

Thank you to our hero Don Brown—we couldn't have done it without you. To Maureen and Steve Witmer, thank you for being the first people we call when we have a crisis! Ron and Alice Vallar—you (and the babies) are the best.

To my fellow rescuers and schnauzer-lovers at www.njsrn.petfinder.org, thank you for giving me the chance to contribute to the greater good without leaving the inn—and for fosters that don't bark too much!

Special thanks to all of the writers who've visited us through the years and helped spread the word—you have been invaluable to our success. And to our suppliers who understand what we're about and always give us their best.

Thank you, Harriet, the grand dame of editing, for sharing my enthusiasm and channeling it into such a beautiful book. Bravo to photographer Ellen Silverman and crew, and stylists Anne Disrude and Betty Alfenito for making my food look good enough to eat. We are grateful to Leah Carlson-Stanisic and Roberto de Vicq de Cumptich for using their extraordinary talents to design this book inside and out.

And finally, thanks to my family for supporting our efforts, and especially to my nephew Matt who at the age of three gave us one of our favorite sayings: "I'm tired of being quiet for the guests!"

Thank you, everyone, for allowing us to live our dream.

INTRODUCTION

My husband, Bob, and I began our careers as innkeepers in the same way I remember first going into the deep end of the pool. It involved a very sophisticated start-up strategy that went something like this: Close your eyes, hold your breath, and jump. After thirteen-plus years as an innkeeper, I am convinced that this "leap of faith" business plan is the only possible approach. In fact, I'm willing to bet that if you've fantasized about owning an inn, your business plan is just as complicated as ours was.

Having a country inn is one of the great fantasies of adult life. The idea of chucking it all—the daily commute, the intense competition, and the technological madness of the working world—is so appealing that many people view owning an inn as the ultimate antidote to life's pressures. Part of that scenario is absolutely true: It certainly does cut out the commute. But the real appeal of owning an inn is based on the

same pleasures derived from other positive aspects of life—the chance to interact with people, to meet new friends and to savor relationships.

Above all, I want the people who stay with us to feel as if they are invited guests rather than paying customers. For me, the first step is to offer my guests a warm and friendly greeting. The second step is to offer them something exceptional to eat. At the Inn at Twin Linden, food is an essential part of the experience we create for our guests. Since we first opened our doors over ten years ago, we've followed a simple motto: If you cook it *well*, they will come. And so they have.

This book details the nuts and bolts of innkeeping as well as the fantasy of it all. Since the food we serve is so much a part of staying at our inn, it also features the recipes that our guests enjoy and

request. As you join me in the day-to-day world of innkeeping, we'll whip up egg dishes for breakfast and set up the sideboard for afternoon tea. I'll share the shortcuts I've learned from preparing these dishes day in and day out. We'll make dinner, we'll plan desserts, and we'll organize our baking for the next morning.

As you might imagine, owning a country inn is about much more than preparing food, so this is where we'll explore the fantasy part of innkeeping. While we prepare some wonderful dishes together, we'll pass some time in the kitchen in my favorite way—we'll talk. I know you're curious about what it's really like to own your own country inn. Is it really hard work? Do you ever get tired of making breakfast? Are most people nice? How about the inn itself—did it look this way when you bought it? Did you think it would look like this *after* you bought it? Did you do all the decorating yourself? Of course it's hard work, but you must love it, right?

Step into the real world of innkeeping. Answer the phones and hear some of the unusual requests made by potential guests. On the way to pick herbs, we'll talk about how our grounds evolved from patches of crabgrass to lush gardens laced with secret paths. While we wander through the guest rooms, we'll talk about neat guests and not-so-neat ones. We'll hire dishwashers and hope they show up for work on a busy Saturday night. While we visit the farm stands, you'll discover eastern Pennsylvania and learn about our Amish and Mennonite neighbors, who still use the horse and buggy as their means of transportation.

We'll talk about how we became innkeepers and what it felt like when the first guests arrived at our door. You'll be with us when we first see the rundown building that will become the Inn at Twin Linden Country Inn. We'll tell you how our dreams of owning our inn almost left us penniless and without a roof over our heads. And I'll share our triumph when our inn was named "One of the Year's Best" by a national magazine.

The fantasy part of innkeeping is much like any other dream; it has less to do with reality and everything to do with possibilities. The possibilities of an inn are limitless, since every element that makes up an inn involves a personal decision by you, the innkeeper. How many rooms will we have? What will the decor be? Where should the antique armoire be placed? What will we serve for breakfast this morning? Owning a country inn is a lot like coming to the fork in the road and having to decide which way to go, over and over again. It begins with a wonderfully delirious moment, when you first imagine yourselves as innkeepers. To be an innkeeper or not to be an innkeeper, that is the first of many questions. And so begins our story, in a small town on the northern Maine coast.

The "Practice" Inn

We are driving down the main street of Eastport, Maine, on a perfectly sunny August day with a crystal clear azure sky. The bustling tourist towns of southern Maine have driven us north to explore the rugged coastline and to escape the crowds. As we read in our guidebook, Eastport had once been a prosperous fishing town. The remnants of wealth are still visible in the beautiful centuries-old homes that line the main street. As we drive toward the oceanfront, we can't help but notice a brightly painted Victorian amidst the otherwise decaying homes, boasting all the requisite bric-a-brac trim and a simple sign: BED AND BREAKFAST. We decide to stay overnight.

As insignificant a moment as this may seem, it marks the beginning of our innkeeper fantasy. From this point on, our lives will forever change course.

Newly married and enchanted with the idea of spending summers together by the ocean, we begin to work out the details. As a university professor in Philadelphia, Bob enjoyed summers off from work. At the time I was a self-employed video producer, so my schedule was somewhat flexible as well. The only hitch was that we didn't have the *money* to spend summers together by the ocean. Still, we tend not to be impeded by the idea that we don't have enough money to do something (you'll see later that this is an important personality trait for innkeepers). Two days later we had agreed to buy a property a few doors down from the place where we were staying and open a B&B. After all, we were staying in one, so why not open an inn ourselves? So it was that our "practice" inn, the Inn at Eastport, came to be.

The Inn at Eastport is key to our fantasy because it gave us an opportunity to experience a little taste of being innkeepers without taking the full plunge. We had risked a lot, but we hadn't invested it all, either financially or emotionally. We still had our home in the Philadelphia suburbs. After one summer of extensive renovations and three summers of running our B&B, we realized that Eastport was not where we wanted to spend the rest of our days. We also realized that our practice inn was not enough to make us happy. We would need to take the big step and have a "real" inn.

A "real" inn meant one we could run full-time and year-round. We had a simple plan: Sell all our belongings, invest everything in one property, and open a first-rate inn. We had little idea what a first-rate inn would look like, since we had stayed in only one B&B before buying our place in Eastport. Our experience in Maine did, however, teach us several important things about innkeeping. First, we would need a property large enough to accommodate a private bath for each room. Second, we would have to live there all the time, since it was difficult for us to go back and forth between two places. Third, we would have to find a place that had an appeal to travelers looking for a respite from their daily lives, yet close enough to an urban area to be reached for a weekend.

So we took a drive. We decided to drive exactly one hour outside of Philadelphia in all directions, making our inn within easy striking distance for a weekend escape from the city. We got off the Pennsylvania Turnpike at Exit 22 in Lancaster County, a rural farming area also known as Pennsylvania Dutch Country. We agreed to drive about five minutes more and turn around, staying within our self-imposed sixty-minute radius. It was a perfect day for a ride, a sunny day in late September when the fall foliage was beginning to show its vibrant colors. What we saw exactly five minutes later would change our lives forever.

Taking the Plunge

A small road marker heading into town announced "ENTERING CHURCHTOWN. NAMED FOR THE PREVALENCE OF CHURCHES." A simple message, but to the point. A collage of church steeples rises above the historic homes, confirming that the town is aptly named. We will come to appreciate that this "plain" talk is a deeply rooted part of the history of this area of rural Pennsylvania. It comes from the society of people who have occupied this farmland since William Penn chartered the property to them in the late 1600s. Those Amish and Mennonites who live here are known as the "Plain People," mostly because of the plain dress they wear. They also adhere to a plain lifestyle, rejecting modern conveniences and using only horse and buggy as a means of transportation. As we enter town, we come up behind one of these slow-moving buggies, clip-clopping at a

steady, even pace. With no passing lanes in town, we are forced to slow down to what seems like a crawl at five miles per hour, which gives us the opportunity to notice a FOR SALE sign to our left.

It's a large three-story building with a white clapboard exterior. The front porch runs the length of the building, with white columns supporting the roof every ten feet or so. We pull off the road to get a closer look. It is apparently deserted, which gives my husband encouragement to peer into the multi-paned windows. Flanked by huge wooden shutters, the window glass is wavy and thick. Inside we can see through to massive paneled doors and worn pine floors. Outside, it appears that the only noticeable landscaping was done more than a hundred years ago. Commanding trees dominate the property, many of them so unusual that we do not recognize the shape of their leaves. Wandering around the back, past the huge red barn (yes, we exclaim to each other, a huge red barn!), the moment occurs that will determine everything we do for the next fifteen years. Before us are a pair of magnificent trees, perfectly symmetrical with trunks ten feet around, spreading their canopy above the three-story building: the twin lindens.

To say we couldn't contain ourselves while we waited for the real estate agent to arrive is beyond understatement. We were choosing the new color for the front shutters as he pulled into the drive. By the time he had unlocked the back door, we had laid out the brick courtyard under the linden trees and were selecting the first wicker chairs for the back porch. We had even chosen a name: the Inn at the Twin Lindens. The agent suddenly disrupted our musings with a stern correction. "Twin Linden," he rebuked, placing enormous emphasis on the "den." "The correct historical name is Twin Linden, as in the *singular*—not lindens. The townspeople will *never* agree to a name change." And so the name of our new inn became historically correct

and grammatically inaccurate. It would be the first of many compromises that would typify our lives as innkeepers in the years to come.

After reviewing our finances, we once again found ourselves in the inconvenient position of knowing what we wanted but not having the money to get it. So we compromised. We sold our house outside of Philadelphia and moved into one of the apartments that the building had been divided into during the early 1960s. (Altogether the building had three huge apartments, one with two bedrooms and two with four bedrooms, each with full bath, kitchen, living room, and dining room.) We would continue to rent the other two apartments until we were able to sell our place in Maine and use the proceeds to do the extensive renovations required to open our new inn.

Twin Linden had languished on the market for more than a year for good reason: it was in terrible condition. Built in the mid-1800s for the daughter of a wealthy forge owner, the property had suffered a serious decline through its various incarnations as estate home, boardinghouse (thirteen rooms with one bathroom, we've been told), a home for the elderly, and now as an apartment building. The roof leaked, the basement flooded, and the septic backed up, and all of this happened on the day we moved in. But like lovers who are blind to each other's imperfections, we didn't even see them. While peeling paint from the back porch ceiling showered us with snowlike flakes, we argued about where the porch swing should go. As we wandered through the empty upstairs bedrooms, still strewn with boxes and other remnants of our move, we discussed where to place the antique bedstead. We walked the perimeter of our 2¾ acres debating the merits of a croquet lawn versus a putting green and never even thought about the size of the mower that would be needed to tame this vast grassland. We made muddy tracks through the barren area under the linden

trees and imagined a lush ground cover, never bothering to consider the cost of the thousands of pachysandra plugs necessary to achieve this effect. When we woke up from the honeymoon, we were overwhelmed. Our bride seemed to have no end to her surprises. One by one the kitchen appliances died. The water softener stopped softening the water. The light fixture in the kitchen flashed madly each time the washer changed cycles. Water ceased flowing from the faucets. We longed to get started on the daunting job before us but were forced to wait while the Inn at Eastport sat on the market.

Trying to not focus on the dismal condition of the property and lagging real estate sales in Maine, we concentrated on learning about the area we had moved into. Bob had kept his day job as a professor but spent his off hours wandering around the countryside, discovering who would craft the finest furniture for our then-imaginary inn dining room, which local Amish woman had access to the finest handmade quilts, and what kind of produce each farm market could offer us. Wherever he went, Bob carried his camera, photographing the beautiful scenery along the one-lane back roads and through the rolling farm valleys. In the meantime, our move had left me with little television or video work unless I was willing to endure a grueling 2½-hour commute to New York. Without my income, we couldn't afford to *stay* at any of the world's finest inns, so I visited them vicariously through the pages of travel magazines and guidebooks, writing endless lists of features that make a first-class hotel or inn.

And then there was the cooking. With not a single decent restaurant within a ten-mile drive, I was insistent that we would need to open a fine-dining restaurant along with offering lodging. The attraction of candlelight dining, combined with our rural location, would make the Inn at Twin Linden a true country inn. (The term "B&B" usually indicates a property that offers only breakfast to its

something about the "best laid plans." More about the evolution of my cooking career later.

We finally sold our property in Maine and began the renovations. With a contract in hand for the sale of the Maine property, we acquired a "swing" loan, laid out a renovation budget on a single sheet of yellow legal paper, and began spending. The initial construction plan included six guest rooms with private baths, a thirty-seat dining room, and a commercial kitchen. We were visited by several different contractors, each with wildly different plans and equally outrageous prices for the work we had described. (Did I mention that we didn't have an architect? I neglected to include one in the budget.) After a series of frustrating meetings and missed appointments, we finally based our selection on my husband's gut feeling about the older soft-spoken gentleman who had arrived last and who was the only one to arrive on time. I later found that Bob chose the man upon whom our entire renovation would depend because he reminded him of his late father. As crazy as his choice may have seemed, it turned out to be the right one.

Our plumber-electrician would make bathrooms where none had existed before, negotiate pipes around two-foot-wide hand-hewn floor beams, and replace miles of worn wiring ready to burst into flame behind hundred-year-old walls. He would also introduce us to a contractor named Don Brown, who would come on the job to handle the carpentry work and seemingly never leave. Don would turn out to be a combination architect, plumber, artist, and overall genius at building absolutely anything. He has been with us ever since, helping us put the finishing touches on the inn and becoming one of our truest friends. Don has won our undying affection by always answering "Yes" when we begin a sentence with "Is it possible to . . . ?"

The installation of our commercial kitchen

overnight guests, while "country inn" denotes a facility that serves dinner to its guests and often to the public as well.) Bob was quick to point out that my experience as a video producer wasn't exactly a substitute for culinary school. Without the time or the finances to head off to the Culinary Institute of America, I embraced the old adage "Those that can, do." I began cooking. Armed with a stack of food magazines and whatever cookbooks I could borrow, I used the two working burners on our kitchen stove to hone my new craft. As someone who had always enjoyed entertaining, I believed I could use the expertise of the world's finest chefs, via the pages of the magazines and cookbooks, to teach me to cook professionally. When the time arrived for me to become the chef of our inn, my own style would be fully developed. Sounds like a plan, right? It makes me think of another adage, required many approvals by the state health department. We had to draw up plans for the layout, detail what appliances would be placed where, and install a vast and expensive array of safety equipment. The prices for the equipment were staggering. The exhaust system alone priced out at about $1,000 per foot. (If I upgraded from a six-burner to an eight-burner range, I would incur an additional $2,000 just for the exhaust system.)

Now that you've had a little taste of the fantasy part of innkeeping, it's time to get started in the kitchen. We've got food to prepare, gardens to tend, and a whole range of people that I really want you to meet. You're about to become an innkeeper with me. It's very simple, really. Close your eyes, hold your breath, and jump. And just one more thing: Welcome to the Inn at Twin Linden. We've been expecting you.

About the Recipes

These recipes are ones that are most requested at the inn and that you might enjoy making at home. I've simplified some of them to accommodate the limited time that many people have to prepare meals. Others require a little more planning, making them ideal for company or special occasions.

There seems to be an all-or-nothing trend in cooking these days. The choice is either to make something quickly prepared but plain or to spend an inordinate amount of preparation time making something that's truly over the top. This approach implies that inventive, interesting food must involve complex preparation. Don't believe it. You can be both inventive *and* practical. Being an innkeeper forces me to do both. I don't have a lot of time to devote to preparing one dish, but I am obligated to present my guests with unique food that

they can't get anywhere else. My goal as chef at the inn is to create a level of complexity that is intriguing to the palate and not overwhelming or time-consuming to prepare.

There are simple ways to accomplish this. First, we all know how important quality ingredients are. Sometimes the simplest dishes are raised to the sublime because of the stellar attributes of the individual components. For example, imagine a plate of summer plum tomatoes and slices of fresh mozzarella, drizzled with extra virgin olive oil and sprinkled with ribbons of fresh basil. You just can't beat a dish like that. Your responsibility as the cook is to gather all the elements together, buying the best quality ingredients possible. If you don't have access to a good local source for produce, this might mean growing your own herbs in a window box or planting tomatoes in a container on your balcony. Many of the exceptional meat products that were once sold only to restaurants are now found in mail-order catalogs and via the Internet. As a home chef, you now often have the same access to these products as the most famous chefs in the country. So when possible, use only the best.

Second, don't overcomplicate the dish. If you're serving a veal chop, let it take center stage. It isn't necessary to add an array of other complicated elements to fill the plate. If you do have several different items on the plate, make sure they're tied together through some common feature. This is what the finest chefs around the world are best at doing—adding only those elements that enhance the inherent quality of the main ingredient.

Finally, believe in your ability to create. To be an inspired chef, you have to muster the will and the confidence to get into the kitchen and literally have at it. Get in there and try things. Some of the best known chefs didn't go to culinary school. Some of the best restaurants offer only fixed menus. So there's no litmus test for being a great chef. You have all the qualifications necessary if you have the enthusiasm to get started and the perseverance to keep trying new things.

All of these recipes can be prepared by you, all by yourself, in your home kitchen. I know this, because I make them all the time—all by myself, in my home kitchen. It's as simple as that. You don't need help to make any of them, although someone to chat with might be nice. You might pass your company a knife and a cutting board and let them chop the onions. These are recipes from a real country inn. I'm hoping you'll enjoy them as much as my guests do.

About Where We Live

Had enough of modern technologies that just seem to make life more complicated? Tempted to purchase one of those how-to-simplify-your-life books and return to less stressful ways? We live among a group of people who've found a way of life that might be just what you're looking for. Here's their basic plan: First, get rid of that cell phone and say good-bye to e-mail. Second, forget about designer clothes; wear black. Third, eliminate your parking woes by selling your car. Sounds like a dream so far, doesn't it? The Amish and Mennonites in our area forgo modern conveniences like cars, telephones, and even electricity, and rely instead on each other. Understanding a little of the history of where our Amish and Mennonite neighbors came from will give you a feeling for the unique area in which we live.

The Amish and Mennonite people of Lancaster County trace their heritage to the Protestant Reformation in sixteenth-century Europe. They began as a single group of religious zealots in Switzerland who had become impatient with what they per-

ceived as the slow pace of the Reformation. They began conferring baptism only on adults who were willing to follow their radical life of strict Christian obedience and thus were nicknamed "Anabaptists," or rebaptizers, since they had already been baptized once in the Catholic Church. The Anabaptist creed included the voluntary submission of one's personal sovereignty for the spiritual betterment of the community. In other words, leave your ego at the door. The movement also rejected the authority of civil leaders. As you might imagine, the authorities did not take too kindly to this rejection. The Anabaptists were persecuted by the thousands and fled to other areas of Europe and eventually to America.

Two sects of Anabaptists, the Amish and the Mennonites, are named for the movement's most influential leaders. The original leader was Menno Simons, a Catholic priest who began to doubt the authority of the Church and whose group of followers became known as Mennonites. A division occurred in the group in the late 1600s, led by a young preacher named Jacob Ammann. Ammann believed that the Mennonites were becoming too lenient. His followers split from the Mennonites to become a distinctive group known as the Amish. To this day, the Amish are considered the stricter group.

The first substantial groups of Mennonites arrived in our area around 1710, attracted by the promise of religious freedom and drawn by the abundance of rich farmland in Lancaster County. Almost thirty years later, the first group of Amish immigrants arrived. Because their native language was a German dialect, the people became known as the Pennsylvania Dutch (a slang interpretation of the word for German, *deutsch*). Today the Amish and Mennonite communities in Lancaster County are among the largest in the country.

The Amish and Mennonites in our area are primarily farmers. Many continue to till the land with

horse-drawn plows in lieu of modern tractors. Because of the limited amount of land available for farming, some men are woodworkers or are employed in other fields that are considered to benefit the group. The women work primarily at home, caring for their large families. They are well known for their quality handcrafted quilts, and they often run the family farm stand in season. Children are taught at an early age how important they are to the family and to the group. This outwardly simple way of living has garnered the Amish and Mennonites the nickname "the Plain People."

Simplicity of dress is the most obvious sign of being "Plain." In its strictest interpretation, the Plain style of dress excludes any item perceived as a decoration or any feature that would make an individual stand out from the group. Even buttons are considered decorative to the Amish, so they fasten their clothes with pins. Amish men and boys wear black suits, while women wear solid-colored dresses. The stricter Mennonites, known as "Old Order," also adhere to an austere but slightly different dress code; they allow muted print fabrics for women and work clothes such as blue jeans for men and boys.

Let me tell you what I perceive as the joys of the Amish and Mennonites. They are raised with an incredible work ethic; they seem to enjoy work instead of merely tolerating it. They appreciate the hard work of others, too. When we completed our initial renovation, our Plain neighbors expressed the greatest appreciation for how much effort had gone into it. They are extremely generous with their time outside their group—for example, volunteering to cook and serve at the local fire company fund-raisers. Their children are well loved and cherished, perhaps because they are seen as blessings rather than as financial burdens requiring college funds or sports cars. They admire the beauty of nature. Our Amish and Mennonite neighbors frequently stop to tour and admire our gardens at the inn. They recycle. They prefer to buy used items at auctions or to bargain for an item at a yard sale rather than purchase something at a store just because it's new. And finally, they like to eat. Growing and sharing food is an important part of their culture. Perhaps we all have more in common than one might have originally imagined.

At the inn, we benefit from being located in an area with the Amish and Mennonites. Our guests take pleasure in the clip-clop of their buggies going by on Sunday morning. They enjoy the bountiful harvest of our local farmers, including the abundance of sweet strawberries in early summer and the tang of freshly pressed cider in autumn. The well kept farms provide a scenic view and the quilt shops a welcome diversion on a Saturday afternoon. Some of our guests return to the inn at day's end, thrilled at their chance encounters with an elderly Amish toy maker who will make a wooden train for a grandchild or a Mennonite woman who will hand-embroider a baby blanket for an expectant mother. In times of need, we have the confidence that the local Plain community will pitch in to help us, as on the Sunday morning when the volunteer firemen delayed attending their religious services to help us put out a fire at the inn. We also appreciate their respectful "live and let live" attitude as neighbors.

Our inn would not be the same without the beautiful place and the admirable community of people in which we live. We are grateful that even in our complicated world, we can enjoy some of the benefits of a simpler way of existence each day, just because of where we have chosen to live.

Photographing the Amish and Mennonites

All of the photographs of our Amish and Mennonite neighbors have been taken with their permission. You may have heard that the Amish and Mennonites do not believe in photography and perhaps are wondering how Bob was able to take photographs of them. The rejection of most photography in the Plain communities has to do with their suppression of individual pride. Photographs that might make someone feel more important than other members of the group are forbidden, but photographs depicting other subjects, such as groups at work or play, are allowed and sometimes even admired.

While the Amish generally do not allow their faces to be photographed, some of our neighbors have allowed Bob to take photographs of their children (they are not baptized until they reach adulthood and thus are not officially church members) or of themselves from behind. Our Mennonite neighbors have also given Bob permission to take photographs with identifiable faces that show their way of life, as opposed to pointing out one individual over another. Some of our Plain neighbors have requested copies of photographs showing their farms or horses. Because Bob's photographs depict our neighbors in a respectful manner, they have given him much more freedom to take photographs of them than they might otherwise have granted. Visitors should *always* ask permission before photographing the Amish and Mennonite people. We hope that these photographs give an insight into the people we regard as our neighbors and an appreciation for the sheer beauty of the scenic farm valleys in which our inn is located.

EGGS

The great taste of fresh eggs is the starting point for some of our guests' favorite breakfast dishes. Our local poultry farmer delivers just-laid eggs to our kitchen door every morning, but not everyone has the luxury of home delivery. Buy your eggs at a busy market to guarantee a fresh supply, and store them on a shelf in the refrigerator (not on the door) in their cartons to maintain their quality.

Eggs have suffered through some unpopular times due to some widely reported misconceptions about dietary cholesterol such as that found in the yolk. Researchers now agree that saturated fat, not the dietary cholesterol level in a particular food, is what raises blood cholesterol. So consuming eggs in moderation is now considered okay for a heart-healthy diet. The popularity of high-protein diets has also helped eggs make a comeback as a favorite morning meal. These recipes use eggs as a starting point for delicious breakfast entrees.

Smoked Salmon
and Goat Cheese Soufflés

I use a good-quality, freshly made goat cheese—the tang asserts itself perfectly against the alder-wood flavor of the smoked salmon. This is a stunning dish for breakfast or brunch, elegant in both presentation and taste.

4 tablespoons unsalted butter	¼ cup all-purpose flour
2 teaspoons chopped shallots	4 large egg yolks
1 cup chopped smoked salmon	2 teaspoons chopped dill
½ cup crumbled goat cheese	6 large egg whites
1¼ cups whole milk	1 teaspoon salt

1. Melt 2 tablespoons of the butter in a medium skillet. Add the shallots and sauté over medium heat until translucent, about 3 minutes. Add the smoked salmon and sauté, stirring constantly, until it lightens in color, about 2 minutes. Distribute the goat cheese evenly over the salmon and set aside to cool slightly.

2. Preheat the oven to 375°F and butter six individual soufflé cups.

3. Heat the milk in a saucepan until just ready to boil.

4. In a medium saucepan, melt the remaining 2 tablespoons of butter. Whisk in the flour and cook for 2 minutes, whisking constantly. Add the hot milk to the flour mixture, stirring vigorously to combine. Continue cooking until the mixture thickens slightly, about 2 minutes. Then whisk in the egg yolks. Continue cooking and whisking until the mixture thickens further, about 2 minutes. Remove the pan from the heat and stir in the dill. Allow to cool slightly, about 5 minutes.

5. With an electric mixer, beat the egg whites with the salt until they form stiff peaks. Fold the salmon mixture into the milk mixture. Gently fold about half the egg whites into the salmon mixture to lighten it. Then gently fold in the remaining egg whites. Divide the soufflé mixture among the six cups. Bake for 20 to 25 minutes or until the soufflés are puffed and golden brown and the centers are set. Serve immediately.

NOTE: The soufflé base may be made up to 2 hours ahead and refrigerated, but don't whisk the egg whites until just before baking. I use tall individual soufflé cups made by Apilco and available through Williams-Sonoma or other fine cookware retailers. If you're using a shorter version, you may want to butter and attach an aluminum foil collar for added height. Remove the collar just before serving.

We sometimes insert a soup spoon into the soufflés tableside (after showing the dramatic presentation to the guests) and then spoon in a little crème fraîche mixed with chopped dill to cool the soufflés slightly before serving.

Smoked salmon comes from a variety of sources. I buy wild Scottish smoked salmon for salads and other dishes, but use other less expensive varieties like Norwegian or Canadian as recipe ingredients. Nova lox (cold-cured salmon) may be substituted for the smoked salmon, but it won't have the same wood-smoked flavor.

Simple Crème Fraîche

MAKES 1 CUP

Crème fraîche is not readily available in our area, so we make our own version. It will not curdle when heated, so it's a perfect addition to soups or other hot dishes requiring a creamy accent. Making crème fraîche requires a little planning, since the ingredients must be assembled at least the night before. It will last up to 2 days under refrigeration.

½ cup sour cream
½ cup heavy cream

Whisk together the sour cream and heavy cream in a metal or glass bowl, and cover with plastic. Allow to ripen at room temperature for at least 12 hours, until the mixture has thickened. Stir the mixture, cover, and refrigerate thoroughly before using.

NOTES FROM THE INN: THE SIGN

The first thing Bob wanted was a sign. Long before the contractors started to create their enormous dust clouds, Bob was scoping out signmakers, hoping for the biggest and most impressive sign to place in front of our run-down building, something that would say OPENING SOON. Somehow the sign made the inn "official" for him. We went to a local signmaker who specialized in inexpensive (of course!) screen-printed versions. We explained our basic needs—inexpensive and large—and sat in his office while he searched out some drawing paper and his sample book.

While we waited, we noticed a poster entitled "Signs of Nantucket," with photos of the beautiful hand-carved signs that are so prevalent in New England. One sign featured an exquisite carved oak tree. When Charlie saw us admiring the poster, he told us he had purchased it while attending a sign-carving workshop in New England. To his disappointment, no one had ever requested a hand-carved sign. We looked at the single oak tree again and imagined two linden trees instead. We sketched out a rough design, and a month later our sign arrived—a large, somewhat inexpensive, and absolutely gorgeous hand carving of the twin lindens. On it Charlie added a temporary sign that read OPENING IN JUNE 1990. Bob was right. It was now official.

Cheddar Soufflé Roll

Asoufflé roll is an airy savory jelly roll, also known as a roulade. Soufflé rolls are ideal for a brunch buffet, since they can be assembled the night before and then baked just before serving.

2½ cups milk

¼ cup unsalted butter

½ cup all-purpose flour

½ teaspoon pepper

5 large eggs, separated

½ teaspoon salt

1¼ cups grated cheddar cheese

3 tablespoons chopped cilantro

½ cup chopped plum tomatoes
(about 3 tomatoes)

---

1. Preheat the oven to 350°F. Grease a 15½ × 10½ × 1-inch jelly roll pan. Line the pan with parchment paper, and then grease the parchment with solid shortening. Line a baking sheet with parchment.

2. Heat the milk in a saucepan until it just comes to a boil.

3. In a large saucepan, melt the butter. Stir in the flour and pepper and cook over low heat, whisking constantly, for 2 to 3 minutes. Add the hot milk, whisking constantly to combine. Cook over medium heat until slightly thickened, 1 to 2 minutes.

4. In a small bowl, whisk together the egg yolks. Stir the yolks into the milk mixture and cook for 5 minutes longer. Remove the pan from the heat and allow to cool slightly, stirring occasionally.

5. Using an electric mixer, beat the egg whites with the salt until they form stiff peaks. Carefully fold the egg whites into the cooled milk mixture. Spread the mixture out in the prepared pan and bake for 15 to 20 minutes, until firm and just lightly browned.

6. Lay a kitchen towel on a work surface and cover it with a piece of parchment paper. Remove the jelly roll pan from the oven and immediately invert it onto the parchment. Roll the towel and soufflé up together, jelly roll style, and allow the baked roll to cool slightly. (Leave the oven on.)

7. Unroll the egg soufflé and sprinkle the cheese, cilantro, and tomatoes over it. Roll up the soufflé without the towel or parchment, and place it on the prepared baking sheet. Cover with aluminum foil. Bake for 8 to 10 minutes, until the cheese has melted and the soufflé roll is heated through. Serve warm.

VARIATIONS: Add cooked sausage or chopped ham. Try different cheeses, such as Brie or Camembert. Add chopped sautéed vegetables, such as asparagus, mushrooms, or onions.

To Salt or Not to Salt

Salt is an acquired taste, so unlike some chefs, I don't feel judgmental about it. It's just that salt is impossible to remove once you've added it. I rarely salt egg dishes, whereas Bob launches a full attack. I may prefer a sprinkling of sea salt on fresh asparagus, but Bob needs each spear to be completely covered with a briny taste. I like to add salt by hand, a little pinch at a time, but Bob prefers the gusto of a freely running shaker. When dining out, I will sometimes comment that a dish is too salty. I have never heard Bob say that. In restaurants that don't put salt shakers on the table, we always ask for one. Salt certainly keeps me from ever stealing any morsel from Bob's plate!

At the inn, we always put salt and pepper shakers on the table, as well as small grinders for those who prefer freshly ground pepper. I add a minimum of salt to most dishes, but I invite you to add salt and pepper as you see fit. Not everyone enjoys salt equally, so when serving others, less rather than more is always the better choice.

Really Hot Plate Coming Up

Did you ever have a waiter tell you not to touch the rim of your plate and you accidentally did it anyway and wanted to scream? It makes sense to serve hot dishes on warm plates and cold dishes on chilled plates, but some restaurants overheat the plates. Make sure your plates never change the temperature of the dish. Plates that are too hot may actually cook the food a little further. Being careful is particularly important with egg dishes and delicate sauces, because the line between properly cooked and overcooked is so thin.

Oven-Puffed Lobster and Brie Custards

SERVES 6

At our Maine inn, our guests were thrilled when we included lobster in breakfast dishes. One favorite was Eggs Lobster Oscar, a version of Eggs Benedict using sautéed lobster instead of Canadian bacon. Since I wasn't sure it would have as much meaning in Pennsylvania Dutch Country, we occasionally served lobster for dinner but never at breakfast. One lobster night in the early days of the restaurant, our commercial oven wouldn't stay lit and we had to send all of our guests out for dinner elsewhere. I developed this recipe to take advantage of all the fresh lobster "leftovers." The response was so positive that I now order extra lobster specifically for this dish. Its elegance belies the easy preparation.

---

6 large eggs

¾ cup heavy cream

½ cup half-and-half

2 teaspoons chopped dill

1 pound cooked Maine lobster meat (about two 1½-pound lobsters), chopped

¼ pound Brie, cut into thin pieces

---

1. Preheat the oven to 400°F. Butter six individual custard cups.

2. In a mixing bowl, whisk together the eggs, heavy cream, and half-and-half. Stir in the dill. Fill each custard cup about half full with the egg mixture. Divide the lobster and Brie pieces evenly among the six cups, and top each cup with the remaining egg mixture. Bake until puffed and just beginning to brown, 15 to 20 minutes. Serve immediately.

VARIATION: Substitute fresh crabmeat or shrimp for the lobster.

NOTE: I don't recommend using frozen lobster meat in any recipe other than as a soup base. It has an unpleasant, chewy texture and a stronger taste than the sweet flavor of fresh lobster meat.

Perfect Scrambled Eggs

It seems like a no-brainer: how to scramble an egg. But how many times have you ordered scrambled eggs only to receive a plateful of rubbery chunks? Keeping the heat on low yields the fluffiest, creamiest results. Here's my basic recipe for perfect scrambled eggs.

3 tablespoons unsalted butter	3 tablespoons heavy cream
12 large eggs	Salt and pepper

Melt the butter over low heat in a large skillet. Whisk the eggs together in a mixing bowl, and add to the skillet all at once. Stir continuously until the eggs are more solid than liquid, 8 to 10 minutes. Add the cream and stir until the eggs are set but still glossy. Season to taste, and serve.

Egg Custard with Morels

SERVES 6

Wild morel mushrooms are available in the springtime. They are uniquely delicious and need little enhancement, especially when featured in this elegant custard. For a special added touch, grate on a little black truffle just before serving.

2 tablespoons unsalted butter	¾ cup heavy cream
¾ cup coarsely chopped morels	½ cup fresh bread crumbs
6 large eggs	1 teaspoon chopped thyme

1. Preheat the oven to 375°F. Butter six individual custard cups or ramekins.

2. Melt the butter in a large skillet. Add the morels and sauté for about 5 minutes, or until softened.

3. In a mixing bowl, whisk together the eggs and heavy cream. Fold in the bread crumbs, thyme, and mushrooms. Divide the mixture among the six custard cups. Place the cups in a 9 × 13-inch baking pan and pour in boiling water until it reaches halfway up the sides of the cups. Bake for 15 to 18 minutes, or until the custards are puffed and the centers are just firm.

NOTE: Morels must be washed thoroughly with several rinses of fresh water before using.

Corn Pudding with Cilantro and Chorizo

This is a delicious blend of cornmeal and eggs flavored with spicy sausage and fresh cilantro. Once baked, it slices into clean wedges perfect for buffet service. The entire dish can easily be prepared the night before, refrigerated, and then baked just before serving. Fresh jalapeño adds a lively accent.

½ pound chorizo sausage, casing removed, meat crumbled

1¼ cups milk

¼ cup unsalted butter

¼ cup chopped scallions

¼ cup all-purpose flour

4 large eggs

½ cup yellow cornmeal

1 cup cooked sweet corn, fresh or frozen

½ cup shredded cheddar cheese

3 tablespoons finely chopped jalapeño peppers (about 2 peppers)

3 tablespoons coarsely chopped cilantro

1½ cups seeded and coarsely chopped fresh plum tomatoes (about 5 large tomatoes)

---

1. Preheat the oven to 350°F. Generously grease an 8- or 9-inch round cake pan with solid vegetable shortening.

2. Sauté the chorizo in a skillet until cooked through and browned, about 5 minutes. Drain on paper towels and set aside.

3. Heat the milk in a saucepan until it just comes to a boil.

4. In a large saucepan, heat the butter over medium heat until just melted. Add the scallions and cook until just soft, about 2 minutes. Add the flour and stir to combine. Add the hot milk and whisk vigorously until well combined. Remove from the heat and allow to cool slightly.

5. Whisk the eggs together in a small bowl. Stir the eggs into the cooled milk mixture. Whisk in the cornmeal. Fold in the sweet corn, sausage, and cheese. Stir in 2 tablespoons of the jalapeño peppers and 2 tablespoons of the cilantro. Spoon the mixture into the prepared cake pan and bake for 25 to 30 minutes, until lightly browned and set in the middle.

6. In the meantime, combine the remaining 1 tablespoon jalapeño pepper, 1 tablespoon cilantro, and the plum tomatoes in a small bowl. Remove the corn pudding from the oven. Cut it into wedges, and spoon the tomato mixture over it. Serve immediately.

NOTES FROM THE INN:
THE CONSTRUCTION

Our guests often ask, "Did the inn always look this way?" Our answer is an emphatic "*No!*" Transforming the dilapidated apartment building we purchased into the luxurious inn we imagined began with six months of demolition and rebuilding. The contractors arrived on a snowy January day, and for a while it seemed they would never leave. Plaster walls were reduced to piles of rubble. Antique floorboards were pulled up, replaced, then pulled up again. Pipes and wires ran in mazes across exposed floor joists. Once the huge Dumpster in our parking lot was emptied, it was almost immediately filled up again.

We began with a basic idea of how we would lay out the rooms, based mainly on existing plumbing and an ever-tightening budget. I scribbled the total amount we had to spend at the top of a yellow legal pad, then subtracted the contractors' estimates, and was left with a puny number for other essentials such as bedding and carpeting, and the vaguer (but fun!) category of decorating. How would we ever manage to fill the inn with antiques and luxury amenities? I divided the remaining funds among the six planned guest rooms and the thirty-seat restaurant and went to work. While the contractors hammered and sawed, I went in search of bargains. I set the alarm clock so I could be the early bird at estate sales and antiques markets. I scoured the discount racks for luxury linens. I made deals with the bedding salesman, the carpet salesman, and anyone else who had something we needed but couldn't quite afford.

While Bob went off to teach at his "day job," I dealt with the day-to-day problems of tearing an enormous house apart. He would arrive at the end of the day to see that walls had moved and bathrooms had appeared, glad to have been spared the seemingly endless stream of decisions that came up in the course of one day. Every fork in the construction road led to added costs and compromises. One day I overheard the contractors admitting to each other that they actually had no idea what the final bill would be.

My typical construction-era days went something like this: Get up at an ungodly hour in order to be dressed and awake when the plumbers arrived. Find out what the basic plan was for the day (installing bathroom fixtures, running electric, or whatever) and determine to what degree I needed to be available. Search out any antiques or other furnishing finds, set up any deliveries, and pile the new acquisitions in the completed common areas. Around midday, check in with the contractors, find out what disasters occurred while I was gone, and generally make any decisions in favor of the cheaper alternative. Late afternoon, find out from the departing crew what areas were completed and begin painting—two or three coats of white on the walls, colonial colors for the woodwork and stenciling. (My painting clothes became a running joke with the crew, basically because I had more paint on me than on the walls.) Clean up from painting and deduct whatever I had spent that day on the legal pad budget. Lie in bed, wide awake, trying to figure out how we are going to pay for everything we still need.

In the end, tile floors were laid. (We bought out all the overruns from an installer, so we had a variety of different styles and colors for about $100.) Beds were assembled and curtains hung. The finished decor represented a blend of the traditional elegance of colonial furnishings and antiques with more sophisticated design elements such as coordinated fabrics and overstuffed chairs. In early June, when the money ran out, we used credit cards to purchase the air conditioners. We had put together the most luxurious country inn in our area, but not nearly at the level we had hoped for. Overall, we were exceedingly proud of everyone's efforts. Over the next ten years, every cent of income would go to making the existing accommodations more luxurious and adding deluxe suites to enhance our offerings. But on opening day in June 1990, with all the pride and excitement of our great construction adventure completed, we had only one thing on our minds: Would we ever have any customers?

Ham and Cheese Pie

My Italian grandmother used to make a pie like this for Easter breakfast. She made her dough by hand, but a food processor also yields good results. It's an excellent addition to a brunch buffet, since it tastes delicious even when served at room temperature.

1¼ cups all-purpose flour	1½ cups diced ham
1 teaspoon salt	½ cup heavy cream
½ teaspoon baking powder	½ cup milk
2 large eggs	3 large eggs
¼ cup extra virgin olive oil	1 cup part-skim ricotta cheese

---

1. First, make the dough for the tart shell: Combine the flour, ½ teaspoon of the salt, and the baking powder in a large bowl. In a small bowl, whisk together the eggs and olive oil. Make a well in the center of the dry ingredients and pour in the egg mixture. Stir the mixture well until it begins to form a dough. Place the dough on a lightly floured surface and knead until smooth, about 1 minute. Roll the dough into a ball and cover it with plastic wrap. Refrigerate the dough for at least 1 hour, or up to 12 hours.

2. When you're ready to make the pie, preheat the oven to 375°F.

3. Roll out the dough on a lightly floured surface, and press it into a 9- or 10-inch tart pan with a removable bottom. Prick the dough with a fork. Sprinkle the ham evenly over the dough. In a large bowl, whisk together the cream, milk, eggs, and remaining ½ teaspoon salt. Pour the egg mixture over the ham. Drop the ricotta by tablespoons evenly over the egg mixture. Bake for about 40 minutes, until the filling is set and slightly puffed. Cool slightly before serving.

VARIATION: For a more sophisticated version, substitute prosciutto for the diced ham and spread the crust with basil pesto before filling.

Prosciutto and Egg Tart in a Polenta Crust

SERVES 6

The crust for this tart is a quick five-minute version of polenta, but instant polenta (which comes in a tube) would work as well.

2½ cups half-and-half
1 tablespoon unsalted butter
1 teaspoon salt
1 cup yellow cornmeal
2 tablespoons mascarpone
2 teaspoons chopped flat-leaf
    parsley

1 tablespoon extra virgin olive oil
2 tablespoons chopped shallots
¼ cup chopped prosciutto
10 large eggs
¼ cup part-skim ricotta cheese
2 tablespoons chopped basil

---

1. Preheat the oven to 350°F. Generously butter a 9- or 10-inch round tart pan with a removable bottom (or use six individual tart pans with removable bottoms).

2. Combine the half-and-half, butter, and salt in a medium saucepan and bring to a boil. Whisk in the cornmeal, a little at a time, until all is combined. Lower the heat and continue cooking, stirring constantly, until the mixture pulls away from the sides of the pan, about 5 minutes. Remove the pan from the heat and stir in the mascarpone and parsley. Press the mixture into the tart pan to form the crust (use the back of a tablespoon, as the mixture will be hot). Bake the crust for 12 minutes (8 minutes for individual pans), until just beginning to turn golden.

3. In the meantime, heat the oil in a large skillet over low heat. Add the shallots and cook until soft, about 2 minutes. Add the prosciutto and cook for 1 minute more. Whisk the eggs together in a large bowl, and add them all at once. Cook, stirring constantly, until the eggs are glossy but still soft. Remove from the heat and stir in the ricotta.

4. Spoon the egg mixture over the crust and bake for 10 minutes, until the eggs are just set. Sprinkle with the basil, cut into wedges, and serve.

NOTE: To add another layer of flavor to this dish, try adding the white wine and pesto sauce on page 162. The crust may be made up to 1 day in advance.

Rising with the Chickens

Guests frequently assume we get up really early to prepare breakfast at the inn, but we don't. I set the alarm for no earlier than six A.M. The key to serving an elegant meal early in the day is having a plan. I know what the menu will be that morning, so we go right to work as soon as we get to the kitchen. Bob starts the coffee (we need this right away!), and I get the baked goods mixed and into the oven. While Bob slices melon, I assemble the entree ingredients. (We have separate work stations, and we joke about not invading each other's space.) In between, we set out coffee and other beverages for the early-rising guests. In season, we wander out to the garden, filling the bird feeders along the way. While I gather fresh flowers for the fruit plates and snip herbs, Bob might pick cherry tomatoes to serve roasted with the frittata. Just before serving, we squeeze the oranges for juice and blend the fruit puree. We go about our jobs, chatting away, drinking coffee, and basically enjoying each other's company. We have a pretty good time.

When our guests ask how we could possibly be ready to put out a sophisticated meal at eight-thirty in the morning, I tell them the truth. Even at the crack of dawn, we like what we're doing and our enthusiasm gives us the energy to get things done. I get to enjoy the beauty of the sunrise and the sound of roosters crowing while I walk to work. "At the very least," I tell our guests, "you just can't beat the commute."

Gorgonzola-Sausage Frittata

Frittatas are among my favorite easy-to-make breakfasts. All of the ingredients may be prepared the night before if desired, then assembled and cooked just before serving. This version features Italian sausage and Gorgonzola, but feel free to try other combinations, such as chorizo and cheddar or even smoked salmon and goat cheese.

2 medium red-skinned potatoes
½ teaspoon salt
4 teaspoons extra virgin olive oil
½ pound sweet Italian sausage,
    casings removed, meat
    crumbled

6 large eggs
1 red bell pepper, sliced
¼ cup crumbled Gorgonzola
¼ cup basil leaves

1. Using a sharp knife or a mandoline, cut the potatoes into thin slices. Place them in a large skillet, and add enough water to just cover the slices. Sprinkle with the salt. Bring the water to a boil and cook the potatoes for 3 to 5 minutes, until just tender. Drain, and allow the potatoes to cool.

2. In a medium frying pan, heat 2 teaspoons of the olive oil over medium heat. Add the sausage and cook until browned and cooked through, 4 to 5 minutes. Remove the sausage from the heat and drain off any fat.

3. In a large bowl, whisk the eggs together until combined.

4. In a medium ovenproof skillet, heat the remaining 2 teaspoons olive oil over medium heat. Add the bell pepper and sauté, stirring often, until just soft, 4 to 5 minutes. Remove the pan from the heat and arrange the potato slices, overlapping slightly, over the peppers. Distribute the cooked sausage and the Gorgonzola evenly over the potato slices. Gently pour the eggs over all.

5. Cover the skillet and return it to low heat. Cook until the eggs are set, 5 to 6 minutes.

6. Meanwhile, preheat the broiler.

7. Place the skillet under the broiler, about 4 inches from the heat, and cook until the eggs are just beginning to brown, about 5 minutes. Remove the skillet from the broiler. Slice the basil into thin ribbons and sprinkle them on top of the frittata. Cut the frittata into wedges and serve warm.

NOTE: I often serve this over a bed of our own garden-fresh mesclun greens drizzled with basil pesto. The dish is best served immediately, but it may be reheated in the oven or microwave as necessary.

The Propane Torch Demo

I do a lot of cooking demonstrations to promote the inn and my cookbooks. One demo was at a fitness fair that was also the sign-up location for a marathon race. Since the accent was on healthy living, I decided to show how to cook a low-fat version of a smoked trout frittata. As frequently happens with demos, there was no real kitchen setup, just a single burner on which to cook. I was in a quandary about how I'd brown the frittata without a broiler, so I decided to bring along a propane torch, the kind plumbers use and also the type chefs use to caramelize the sugar on crème brûlée.

As the marathon runners milled around the various booths, the announcer gave an animated blow-by-blow description over the loudspeaker of what I was cooking. I think he felt sorry for me, because no one was really paying attention. When he announced that I had pulled out the propane torch and was now about to brown the frittata, it was like a magnet—the mostly male crowd gathered around me, completely fascinated. The idea of cooking with a hardware item was too much for them to resist. I handed out samples, and everyone raved about them and talked about how they never knew you could cook with a blowtorch. I didn't want to spoil everything by telling them a broiler would give much better results.

Asparagus and Sweet Onion Tart

SERVES 6

Nothing says springtime in our area like the sight of our Plain farmers applying a fresh coat of white paint to their farm stands and putting out FOR SALE signs for their first crop, asparagus. From the time the harvest begins to the last sad day when the signs disappear, we serve asparagus in its many wonderful incarnations, among them this tasty egg tart. I often use puff pastry dough for a flaky, buttery tart crust.

---

1 recipe Simple Puff Pastry (see recipe following)	4 ounces goat cheese
½ pound asparagus spears	3 large eggs
2 tablespoons unsalted butter	1 cup half-and-half
2 cups sliced sweet onions	½ teaspoon white pepper

---

1. Preheat the oven to 375°F.

2. Roll out the puff pastry to approximately ¼ inch thickness, and fit it into a 10-inch round tart pan with a removable bottom. Trim off any excess and save for another use. Line the pastry with parchment paper or aluminum foil, and add pie weights or dried beans. Bake for 15 minutes, pressing down with a spatula if necessary to keep the pastry from puffing up.

3. In the meantime, bring lightly salted water to a boil in a large skillet. Add the asparagus and cook until bright green and just tender, 3 to 5 minutes depending on the thickness of the spears. Immediately drain the asparagus and submerge them in ice-cold water.

4. Melt the butter in a large skillet. Add the onions and cook until softened and just beginning to turn golden, 10 to 12 minutes.

5. Drain the asparagus and chop into 1-inch pieces. Spread the onions in the bottom of the baked tart shell. Distribute the asparagus evenly over the onions. Crumble the goat cheese over the asparagus. Whisk together the eggs, half-and-half, and pepper in a mixing bowl, and pour over all. Bake for 25 minutes, until set and just beginning to brown. Cool slightly before slicing to serve.

VARIATION: Use different cheeses, such as Brie or fontina.

NOTE: Substitute one 10 × 14-inch sheet of store-bought puff pastry for the homemade version if desired. The tart may be prepared up to 2 hours ahead and reheated in a 350°F oven for 5 minutes.

Simple Puff Pastry

one cup (2 sticks) cold unsalted butter
1⅓ cups all-purpose flour
½ teaspoon salt

1. Cut the butter into ¼-inch pieces. Place 1⅓ cups of the flour and the ½ teaspoon salt in a food processor and add ¼ cup of the butter pieces, pulsing until combined. In a mixing bowl, toss the remaining ⅓ cup flour with the remaining butter pieces until the butter is coated with flour. Add the remaining butter pieces to the food processor and pulse two or three times to just combine. Add ⅓ cup water and pulse until the dough just forms a ball.

2. Dust a work surface with flour and roll out the dough to form a 10 × 14-inch rectangle. Fold the dough into thirds, creating a 3 × 14-inch rectangle. Fold into thirds again, this time forming a 3 × 4-inch rectangle. Wrap it in plastic wrap, and refrigerate for at least 1 hour. (The dough may be refrigerated for up to 2 days or frozen for up to 1 month.)

3. Roll out the dough on a lightly floured surface to the desired degree of thickness.

DRESSED-UP EGGS

Here are some simple ideas for dressing up egg dishes:

• Melt 2 tablespoons butter in a large skillet, then add 1 cup finely chopped mushrooms and sauté briefly until softened. Stir in ¼ cup heavy cream and bring just to a boil. Spoon over poached eggs and serve with toast points.

• Reduce 1 cup white wine to a few tablespoons. Add ½ cup heavy cream and reduce until thickened, about 5 minutes. Stir in chopped fresh herbs (parsley, dill, chives, cilantro), mustard, or pesto. Spoon over egg-filled crepes.

• Whisk together crème fraîche and fresh herbs, then spoon into a squeeze bottle to garnish any egg dish.

• Make a simple salsa by tossing together 1 cup chopped plum tomatoes, 1 teaspoon chopped jalapeño pepper, 2 tablespoons chopped scallions, and 1 tablespoon chopped basil or cilantro. Sprinkle around the edge of the dish to enhance egg tarts.

• Blend ½ cup roasted red bell peppers and ¼ cup fresh tomato sauce in a food processor or blender until smooth. Warm the coulis and serve it on the side, in a small pitcher or gravy boat, with slices of rolled omelet or soufflé roll.

• Whisk together ½ cup crème fraîche and ½ ounce caviar. Dot the mixture around the edge of the plates for an elegant touch on perfect scrambled eggs.

• Cut cherry tomatoes in half, toss with extra virgin olive oil, and roast in a 375°F oven for 5 to 7 minutes. Sprinkle with fresh basil and serve as a side dish for a frittata.

Baked Eggs with Caramelized Onions

SERVES 6

Caramelizing onions intensifies their inherent sweetness. Naturally sweet onions yield the best results, so use Vidalia or Walla Walla if they're in season. I've also made this dish with home-grown baby leeks, but don't substitute the full-grown ones, as their sugar won't be concentrated enough to bring out the flavor in this dish.

---

6 slices Simple Brioche Loaf
(page 62) or challah
2 tablespoons unsalted butter
4 cups sliced sweet onions

6 large eggs
¼ cup heavy cream
2 tablespoons chopped chives

---

1. Preheat the oven to 350°F. Butter six ramekins or custard cups.

2. Toast the brioche or challah slices until just golden. Keep warm.

3. Melt the butter in a large skillet. Add the onions and cook over medium heat, stirring often, until golden and caramelized, 12 to 15 minutes. Remove from the heat and keep warm.

4. Crack an egg into each ramekin. Place about 1 teaspoon of the cream on top of each egg. Place the ramekins in a baking pan and fill the pan with hot water until it reaches two-thirds the way up the sides of the ramekins. Bake the eggs for 5 minutes for soft yet firm yolks, or until the eggs reach the desired degree of doneness.

5. Place a piece of toast on each plate, and spoon the onions over the toast. Make a well in the center of the onions. Using a tablespoon, scoop a baked egg into each well. Sprinkle with the chives and serve immediately.

NOTE: If sweet onions are unavailable, some chefs add 1 to 2 tablespoons of sugar to large white onions to aid the caramelization process.

Springtime at the Inn Means . . .

Visiting reopened farm stands to buy fresh asparagus.

Clearing out the mulch from the flower beds and raking up any leaves left from fall.

Breathing new life into menus with spring vegetables.

Cleaning out the birdhouses to welcome new inhabitants (or sometimes returning ones).

Adding composted fertilizer to the flower and vegetable beds and turning the soil.

Trimming the raspberries, blackberries, and gooseberries.

Picking fresh sorrel and chives for breakfast dishes.

Enjoying the waves of blossoms from bulbs diligently planted over many fall seasons past.

Spraying the roses and fruit trees with dormant oil to eliminate overwintering diseases.

Planting seeds and tending the tiny plants growing in the basement
that will become our summer garden.

Drying freshly washed comforters in the balmy spring breezes.

Planting lettuces, mâche, fava beans, and peas in the raised beds.

Replacing storm inserts with screens and enjoying fresh air once again.

Closing the windows when farmers spread manure on their fields.

Smoked Salmon and Eggs with Sorrel

SERVES 6

Sorrel is a lemon-scented, leafy perennial herb that flourishes in cool spring weather. When I was planting the inn's first herb garden, I included sorrel but had no plan for how I'd use it. In a year's time, it became so prolific that it demanded my culinary attention. After trying different preparations, I've found that sorrel is best when cooked briefly in butter and finished with a touch of cream. Its naturally complex taste will have your guests wondering how you made this delightfully simple sauce. If sorrel is unavailable, tender young spinach makes a good substitute.

12 sorrel leaves	12 slices smoked salmon
2 tablespoons unsalted butter	2 tablespoons distilled white
¼ cup heavy cream	vinegar
6 slices Simple Brioche Loaf	6 large eggs
(page 62) or challah	3 tablespoons chopped chives

1. Slice the sorrel into thin ribbons. Melt the butter in a medium skillet. Add the sorrel and cook just until it wilts, about 2 minutes. Add the cream and bring to a boil. Continue cooking until sauce is slightly thickened, about 3 minutes. Remove the skillet from the heat and keep warm.

2. Preheat the broiler.

3. Toast both sides of the bread until just golden. Place the salmon slices on a broiler pan and broil 2 to 3 inches from the heat until just beginning to brown, about 1 minute per side. Keep warm.

4. Fill a large skillet with about 2 inches of water. Add the vinegar and bring to a boil. Gently break the eggs into the water, one at a time. Reduce the heat to a simmer and poach the eggs for 3 minutes. Remove the eggs with a slotted spoon, and briefly submerge them in hot water to rinse off any residual vinegar taste.

5. Place a slice of toast on each plate, and top each with 2 slices of smoked salmon. Gently place an egg on top. Divide the sorrel sauce among the six servings, and garnish with the chives. Serve immediately.

NOTE: Don't be hesitant to try poaching eggs. It's an easy process, merely requiring a gentle touch. The cooked eggs can even be held briefly in very warm water until all are poached.

Mediterranean Eggs

Tapenade, the zesty Provençal spread of olives, garlic, and anchovies, is the inspiration for this dish. The poached egg breaks over the eggplant filling and incorporates all the flavors. If you prefer not to use poached eggs, scramble or hard-boil the eggs instead. Add crusty French bread and fragrant extra virgin olive oil, and you'll almost believe you're in the South of France.

---

6 baby eggplants, 5 to 7 inches long	One 2-ounce can anchovy fillets,
3 tablespoons extra virgin	drained and minced
olive oil	1 cup chopped plum tomatoes
1½ teaspoons minced garlic	(about 3 tomatoes)
½ cup calamata olives, pitted and	2 tablespoons distilled white
finely chopped	vinegar
¼ cup small capers, drained	6 large eggs

---

1. Preheat the oven to 350°F.

2. Place the eggplants on a baking sheet and bake for 35 to 45 minutes, until beginning to soften. Allow the eggplants to cool. Then slice them in half lengthwise and remove the flesh, leaving six of the skins intact. Coarsely chop the flesh and set it aside. Place the reserved skins on a baking sheet.

3. Heat the oil in a large skillet. Add the garlic and cook for 30 seconds. Add the olives, capers, and anchovies, and cook for 30 seconds. Remove the skillet from the heat and stir in the plum tomatoes and the reserved chopped eggplant. Divide the mixture evenly among the six eggplant skins. Cover with foil and bake for 20 minutes. Remove the eggplants from the oven and discard the foil.

4. Fill a large skillet with about 2 inches of water. Add the vinegar and bring to a boil. Gently break the eggs into the water, one at a time. Reduce the heat to a simmer and poach the eggs for 3 minutes. Remove the eggs with a slotted spoon and briefly submerge them in hot water to rinse off any residual vinegar taste.

5. Make an indentation in the middle of the filling in each eggplant, and place a poached egg in it. Serve immediately.

NOTE: The snowy white eggplants we grow in our garden have a mild flavor that perfectly balances the tomatoes and olives in this dish. Traditional purple-skinned eggplants may be bitter and sometimes benefit from a sprinkling of kosher or coarse sea salt about 1 hour before using: Set the salted diced eggplant in a colander over a bowl to allow the bitter juices to drain out; then rinse before using.

About Dietary Restrictions

We ask our guests to inform us before they arrive if they have any dietary restrictions, and many of them do. The most common are lactose intolerance, sugar or alcohol restrictions, or a preference for a vegetarian or low-fat meal. Sometimes these restrictions are stringent (people with nut and shellfish allergies can go into shock if these ingredients are mistakenly added), and sometimes they are less strict (some people with adult-onset diabetes still enjoy the chocolate dessert after dinner).

It's helpful to me as the chef, and to anyone hosting guests with dietary concerns, if they are as specific as possible about what they can and cannot eat. The most ambiguous term is "vegetarian" since it means so many different things to different people. When I do a little probing, I've found that many people who call themselves "vegetarian" actually aren't; they merely don't eat red meat. One of my dinner guests once handed the waitress a printed note for me. It read, "I am relying on you to help me not get sick. I am trusting that you will not include any of the following ingredients that will make me very ill," and it went on to list the individual items, such as peppers and garlic. I found this list incredibly helpful when preparing the meal because the diner clearly told me what to leave out; I didn't have to interpret anything. I also realized how much we trust our food providers to not put our health at risk. So when indicating dietary restrictions, do yourself and your host a favor: Give as much advance notice as possible and be specific about your needs.

Risotto and
Egg Casserole

Combining pancetta, shiitake mushrooms, and creamy risotto with eggs takes this casserole from ordinary to sublime. If you prefer a meatless version, leave out the pancetta (the tasty Italian version of bacon) and substitute vegetable stock for the chicken stock. Enjoy this for lunch or dinner, too.

---

6 thin slices pancetta

2 tablespoons unsalted butter

¼ cup chopped onions

1 cup sliced shiitake mushrooms

6 cups Basic Chicken Stock
(page 87)

3 tablespoons extra virgin olive oil

1½ cups Italian medium-grain rice,
such as Carnaroli or Arborio

½ cup dry white wine

9 large eggs

3 tablespoons coarsely chopped
flat-leaf parsley

18 to 24 large shavings Parmesan

---

1. Sauté the pancetta in a large skillet over medium heat, turning over, until browned, 8 to 10 minutes. Drain on paper towels, chop into small bits, and set aside.

2. Melt the butter in a medium skillet. Add the onions and mushrooms and cook until soft, about 3 minutes. Set aside.

3. Bring the chicken stock to a simmer in a medium saucepan, then set it over very low heat.

4. Heat the oil in a large skillet. Add the rice and stir until coated. Cook for 2 minutes longer. Add the wine and immediately reduce the heat to medium (the liquid should be at a steady but gentle bubbling). Stir the rice constantly until all the liquid is absorbed. Ladle in 1 cup of the hot stock and continue stirring until the liquid is absorbed. Continue adding hot stock, ½ cup at a time, stirring often, until the rice is creamy and just tender, about 25 minutes. Remove from the heat.

5. In the meantime, preheat the oven to 350°F. Grease a 2-quart soufflé or casserole dish with solid vegetable shortening.

6. Whisk the eggs together in a mixing bowl, and stir into the rice. Fold in the pancetta, onions and mushrooms, and parsley. Spoon the rice mixture into the prepared dish and bake for 15 to 20 minutes, until cooked and heated through. Spoon the casserole into warmed shallow bowls, sprinkle with the Parmesan shavings, and serve.

VARIATION: Try adding blanched asparagus tips, or using different combinations of herbs and cheeses, such as basil with Gorgonzola.

NOTE: If you prefer to use canned chicken broth, use 3 cups broth and 3 cups of water. To boost the flavor of canned broth, simmer some chopped vegetables (carrots, onion, celery) in it for about 20 minutes before using.

Crab and Eggs in Chive Crepes

SERVES 6

Traveling in France is one of my greatest culinary inspirations. The French have a way of taking something that seems simple, almost a cliché, such as a crepe, and transforming it into a delightful meal. Our travels in Brittany inspired me to revisit crepes at the inn and to come up with this new version of an old favorite.

¾ cup all-purpose flour

7 large eggs

1 large egg yolk

½ cup half-and-half

3 tablespoons chopped chives plus
    18 whole chives

1 tablespoon corn oil or nonstick
    cooking spray

2 tablespoons unsalted butter

½ pound jumbo lump crabmeat

2 tablespoons distilled white
    vinegar

½ cup Simple Crème Fraîche
    (page 17)

---

1. Place the flour in a large mixing bowl and create a well in the center. In another mixing bowl, whisk together 1 egg, the egg yolk, half-and-half, ½ cup water, and chopped chives. Pour this mixture into the well and whisk to combine.

2. Preheat a 7- or 8-inch crepe pan or skillet over high heat, and brush it with some of the oil. Pour in approximately ¼ cup of the batter and swirl it quickly to cover the surface of the pan. Cook over medium heat until the crepe loosens and the edges begin to curl, about 2 minutes. Flip to the other side and cook for a few seconds. Remove the crepe from the pan and place it on a cooling rack. Continue until 6 crepes are completed. Keep the crepes warm in foil.

3. Melt the butter in a large skillet. Add the crabmeat and cook until just heated through, 3 to 4 minutes.

4. Fill a large skillet with about 2 inches of water. Add the vinegar and bring to a boil. Gently place the remaining 6 eggs, one at a time, into the water. Reduce the heat to a simmer and poach the eggs for 3 minutes. Then remove them with a slotted spoon, and briefly submerge them in hot water to rinse off any residual vinegar taste.

5. Place the crepes on individual plates. Place a portion of crabmeat and crème fraîche on the lower third of each crepe. Place an egg on top, and fold the crepe in half. Garnish with the whole chives, and serve.

NOTE: Crepes may be made up to 24 hours in advance. Layer them with waxed paper and seal them in an airtight container until ready to use. Reheat the crepes in foil in a warm oven before filling.

Wilted Spinach and Gorgonzola Omelet Roll

Omelet rolls are a little less time-consuming than soufflé rolls, because you simply combine the ingredients and pour them into the prepared pan to bake. The spinach and Gorgonzola filling adds a sophisticated flavor to a simply prepared dish.

1 cup milk	2 tablespoons extra virgin olive oil
6 large eggs	1 teaspoon minced garlic
½ cup all-purpose flour	1 pound spinach, washed and
¼ cup unsalted butter, melted	stemmed
2 teaspoons chopped parsley	¼ cup crumbled Gorgonzola

1. Preheat the oven to 400°F. Grease a 15½ × 10½-inch jelly roll pan with solid shortening. Line it with parchment paper and grease again.

2. Whisk the milk, eggs, flour, and butter together in a mixing bowl until well combined and frothy. Stir in the parsley. Pour into the pan and bake for 18 to 20 minutes, until the roll is just set and slightly puffed.

3. In the meantime, heat the oil in a large skillet. Add the garlic and cook for 30 seconds. Add the spinach and cook for about 2 minutes, until just wilted.

4. Remove the roll from the oven. (Leave the oven on.) Spread the wilted spinach evenly over the roll, and sprinkle the Gorgonzola over it. Roll up the omelet without the parchment, and return it to the oven for 3 to 5 minutes, until the cheese is just melted. Slice into 6 pieces to serve.

NOTES FROM THE INN:
THE GARDENS

We purchased the inn with its only landscaping having been done about a hundred years before. There were the beautiful, often rare, trees that rose above our three-story roof. There was some grass. There were a lot of weeds. There were those large bare spots under the tree canopies.

One of our first projects was to plant ground cover on the shady bare spots. We planted literally thousands of plugs of pachysandra and ivy. A small fountain set on a little brick square in the middle of the yard looked lonely, so Bob went to plant auctions at the local nurseries and bought shrubs. Boxwood hedges were placed to form the future formal garden. Rhododendrons and azaleas took the place of weedy plots. Bob picked up shade-loving bargains such as hostas and ferns. And then there were the mystery plants.

Since Bob couldn't pass up a deal, we had no idea what some of the plants would look like once grown. We gave them names, such as "Green Things" and "Pointy Green Things." They are now some of our most beautiful and unusual plants. Bob also had a Charlie Brown weakness for poor little pathetic plants at discount prices. We placed these close to the property borders so they wouldn't garner much attention while they decided to live or die. I refer to these areas as "Bob's Home for Misfit Plants." Most of them have survived and flourished in our rich soil.

On a warm February day during the initial construction, we hand-dug a 12 by 12-foot area for a brick courtyard, because we were afraid a backhoe would sever the roots of the linden trees—we already had the Twin Linden sign, so what would we do if we lost one or both of the trees? Later our contractor added a cedar trellis over the courtyard with white classical columns to support it. We've been training wisteria over it for years. In season, we set out wrought-iron tables and chairs so guests may enjoy iced tea there in the afternoon or an aperitif before dinner. We've designed rock- and brick-lined paths with red gravel to connect all of the garden spaces.

Our gardens give our guests and us such great pleasure. It's a thrill to show people around to the enclosed porches where we serve breakfast and dinner and to hear them gasp at the sheer beauty of the garden view. Our guests often picnic under the magnificent cherry tree that overlooks the farm valleys behind the inn. It's a parklike setting with garden gates and arbors that draw you from one area to the next. Each new garden room yields a surprise: Exquisite climbing roses lead to lavender hedges, and then on to herb gardens enclosed by rows of tiny boxwoods, and so on.

Our latest addition to the gardens has been an area surrounded with picket fence in which we grow vegetables and berries. We designed it to be a limited space, to prevent our enthusiasm from leading us to grow more than we could use. It features four raised beds for vegetables, a circular bed in the center with French lavender and alpine strawberries, and several rows of raspberries, blackberries, gooseberries, and currants. As aesthetically pleasing as it is functional, the garden allows us to grow varieties not readily available at the local farm stands—delicate lettuces and mâche, chervil, baby leeks, fava beans, haricots verts, and heirloom tomatoes. Outside the pickets is a cutting garden, supplying fresh flowers for the guest rooms. Nasturtiums cover the fence, and a brilliant array of sunflowers towers behind the berries. The surrounding outer beds are planted with perennial vegetables, such as beautiful scarlet asparagus spears and spiky artichokes.

Bob still goes to the plant auctions, but he tries to be more discerning in his purchases. We just don't have a lot of open space left in which to plant! It's amazing, though, how a garden is such a dynamic thing—there are always areas that need to be refreshed or changed. It's really a lot like the inn. I'm not sure we'll ever be at the point where we feel it's "finished." The gardens help make the inn an oasis for our guests. They're also a beautiful and persuasive argument for unrestricted bidding on "Green Things" and other misfit plants.

BREAKFAST FARE

Breakfast has always been an important part of what we offer our guests. When we first opened the inn, we offered a fixed menu, but we soon realized that some people needed a choice. Now, we offer guests a low-fat option (cereal with skim milk) or plain à la carte selections such as eggs or French toast. We refer to our fixed menu option as the "Chef's Deluxe Breakfast." It consists of a warm-from-the-oven baked item, a fresh fruit plate, and a positively decadent entree. Sometimes guests watching their diets may choose a low-fat option, and others who prefer standard breakfast fare may select eggs or French toast. But most of our guests know our reputation for great breakfasts and choose the Chef's Deluxe. It's also not uncommon for someone who first selects a plain meal to decide to switch after seeing his or her partner savor the specialty of the house!

Strawberry Fizz

SERVES 6

Fresh strawberries blended with orange juice are topped off with bubbly club soda. Champagne may be substituted for the club soda if desired. Chill all the ingredients thoroughly before blending.

---

4 cups strawberries, hulled and
quartered (about 2 quarts)
1 cup fresh orange juice

1 liter chilled club soda
Fresh mint, for garnish

Combine the strawberries and orange juice in a food processor or blender, and process until smooth. Stir in the club soda, garnish with the mint, and serve.

The Inn Kitchen

Guests who tour our kitchen are amazed at how we produce our meals in such a compact space. Our kitchen is a basic commercial setup consisting of the following:

- a six-burner gas range with a single gas convection oven

- an infrared salamander broiler (the infrared panels sear meat and seafood more quickly and evenly than a standard open-flame broiler)

- a single-door refrigerator

- an under-counter dishwasher next to a rinse sink

- a small undercounter freezer with a stainless worktop

- a microwave (handy for certain tasks like melting butter)

- five sinks for pot scrubbing, prepping, and hand washing

- three stainless-steel work tables

- a fire suppression system over the range

Very Berry Smoothie

Fresh summer berries provide the basis for this creamy drink, but frozen berries may be substituted as well.

---

1 cup blackberries	1 cup blueberries
1 cup raspberries	2 cups fresh orange juice
¼ cup fresh lemon juice	Sugar to taste
2 cups strawberries, hulled and quartered (about 1 quart)	1 cup low-fat yogurt

---

Combine the blackberries, raspberries, and lemon juice in a blender and process until smooth. Press the mixture through a fine-mesh sieve to remove the seeds. Return the seedless mixture to the blender and add the strawberries, blueberries, and orange juice. Blend until smooth. Add the sugar, 1 tablespoon at a time, processing until smooth each time, until sweetened to taste. Add the yogurt and process until smooth. Serve chilled.

Sparkling Melon Ball

The tang of ginger balances the sweetness of the melon in this effervescent drink. Serve this in tall champagne flutes for an elegant presentation.

---

2 honeydew melons
¼ cup fresh orange juice
1 liter chilled ginger ale

Remove the rind from the melons and cut the fruit into chunks. Combine the honeydew and orange juice in a food processor or blender, and process until smooth. Stir in the ginger ale and serve.

NOTE: Garnish the drink with fresh orange slices skewered to melon balls if desired. This makes a delightful breakfast or brunch buffet punch.

Orange Peach Breakfast Juice

Using ripe seasonal peaches adds a juicy sweetness to this summertime breakfast drink.

---

6 very ripe peaches, peeled, pitted, and sliced
½ cup peach nectar
2½ cups fresh orange juice

Combine the peaches, nectar, and orange juice in a food processor or blender, and process until smooth. Serve chilled.

VARIATION: Add peach schnapps for an alcoholic version.

Flowers for Breakfast

We grow fresh pansies, nasturtiums, and calendula in our gardens to garnish our breakfast plates. I decorate the fresh fruit plate with pansies, because I find they add the least flowery flavor yet the best visual effect. Although it may seem like a small gesture, the simple addition of a colorful pansy brings such a look of pleasure to so many of our guests that I always find time to run out to the garden just before breakfast to pick them. Presentation matters when it comes to making food look enticing, so I take the time to arrange the fruit in an appealing way, adding a little swirl of fruit puree for a dramatic effect and garnishing with pansies for a finishing touch.

Many of our guests ask if the pansies are edible. Somehow, sitting in the beautiful garden setting and enjoying our delicious breakfast must make the timid become bold, because many actually do eat them. Some guests take them home as a memento of their stay. But perhaps the greatest compliment is when guests take out their camera and photograph our fresh fruit plate. It reminds me how important it is to be purposeful in every detail of a dish. Even something as simple as an array of fresh fruit, when treated with a creative eye and enhanced with a perfectly formed pansy, can be regarded as culinary art.

Grapefruit Pineapple Breakfast Juice

SERVES 6

Using ruby red grapefruit will give this drink a soft pink hue. The pineapple adds a little sweetness.

2 cups fresh grapefruit juice
1 cup pineapple juice

Combine the grapefruit and pineapple juices in a food processor or blender, and process until frothy. Serve chilled.

NOTE: If you like, garnish with pineapple slices and grapefruit wedges.

Peach Smoothie with Blueberry Swirl

SERVE 6

Low-fat yogurt gives our smoothies their creamy texture. The swirl of fresh blueberry contrasts with the light peach tint of the smoothie.

6 ripe peaches, peeled, pitted, and
sliced
2 cups peach nectar
1 cup low-fat yogurt

1 cup blueberries
1 tablespoon fresh lemon juice
2 tablespoons honey

Combine the peaches, nectar, and yogurt in a food processor or blender, and process until smooth. Divide the mixture among six glasses. Combine the blueberries, lemon juice, and honey in a bowl, and stir until smooth. Swirl a tablespoon of the blueberry mixture into each glass of peach smoothie, and serve.

NOTE: Refrigerate all the ingredients before blending.

Summer Fruit Parfait

This quintessential summer parfait incorporates sweet melon with layers of minty yogurt flavored with blueberries.

---

2 pints blueberries

2 tablespoons fresh lemon juice

3 tablespoons sugar (or to taste)

2 tablespoons finely chopped fresh mint plus 6 whole sprigs

1 cup low-fat yogurt

Six 1½-inch-thick slices cantaloupe

Six 1½-inch-thick slices honeydew

---

1. Chill six parfait or other deep stemmed glasses.

2. Combine 1½ pints of the blueberries, the lemon juice, sugar, chopped mint, and yogurt in a food processor or blender, and process until smooth. Spoon 2 tablespoons of this mixture into the bottom of each glass. Cut the cantaloupe into 1-inch chunks, and layer then evenly over the blueberry mixture. Spoon another 2 tablespoons of the blueberry mixture over each layer of cantaloupe. Cut the honeydew into 1-inch chunks and layer then evenly over the blueberry mixture. Divide the remaining blueberry mixture among the glasses. Top each parfait with some of the remaining whole blueberries, and garnish with a mint sprig.

NOTE: Make sure your glasses are heavy enough to avoid breakage. We use barware-quality parfait or martini glasses for parfaits or mousses.

Summertime at the Inn Means . . .

Serving tea iced instead of hot.

Grilling fresh seafood instead of roasting meats.

Hearing the gentle squeak of the porch swing.

Having so many fresh herbs to choose from.

Picking our own fresh tomatoes and eating them straight from the vine.

Watering the vegetables and keeping a vigilant eye out for pests.

Sitting in the shade gardens and enjoying the smell of the cool, earthy air.

Collecting linden flowers for potpourri and tea.

Watching the piles of fresh melons at farm stands rise and the prices drop.

Cutting lavender wands and hanging the fragrant bunches for drying.

Discussing rainfall amounts with the local farmers.

Inundating guests with the bounty of our vegetable gardens.

Watching the horse-drawn wagons go by, with children letting their bare feet hang off the sides.

Listening to the clicking cicadas and watching fireflies light up the valley.

Picking abundant flower bouquets from the cutting gardens.

Inviting guests to come inside the picket gate and try some fresh berries.

Sitting on the back stoop in the early evening and shucking sweet corn.

Hoping it will soon get cool enough to open the windows in the inn and
turn off the air-conditioning.

Citrus Fruit Parfait

It's a challenge to create a tasty fresh fruit dish during the winter season. This parfait combines widely available citrus fruits with a sweetened puree of frozen raspberries. We grow lemon verbena in our herb garden and bring the pots inside before the first frost so we can harvest it all winter long. Substitute fresh mint sprigs if verbena is unavailable.

1 cup frozen raspberries
2 tablespoons fresh lemon juice
2 tablespoons sugar (or to taste)
3 tablespoons chopped lemon
    verbena or mint

3 oranges, peeled and sliced into
    chunks
2 grapefruits, peeled and sliced into
    chunks
6 sprigs lemon verbena or mint

1. Chill six parfait or other deep stemmed glasses.

2. Combine the raspberries, lemon juice, and sugar in a food processor or blender, and process until slushy but not smooth. Stir in the chopped lemon verbena. Divide half the raspberry mixture among the glasses. Divide half the oranges and then half the grapefruit chunks among the glasses. Repeat all the layers. Garnish with the lemon verbena sprigs, and serve.

Tropical Fruit Parfait

SERVES 6

Fresh tropical fruits are available during the winter season and are often better quality than out-of-season fruits like strawberries or melons. The mango cream also makes a delicious dip for a fresh fruit platter.

---

1 mango, peeled and pitted

1 cup sour cream

1 pineapple

6 kiwi, peeled and cut into chunks

2 bananas, peeled and cut into
  chunks

¼ cup shredded coconut, toasted
  (see Note)

1 star fruit, ends trimmed, cut
  evenly into 6 slices

---

1. Chill six parfait or other deep stemmed glasses.

2. Combine the mango and sour cream in a food processor or blender, and process until smooth.

3. Cut three ¼-inch-thick slices from the center of the pineapple. Cut each slice in half, remove the center core, and reserve the slices for the garnish. Remove the flesh from the remaining pineapple and cut it into chunks. Toss the pineapple with the mango cream.

4. Divide half the kiwi among the six glasses. Top with half the bananas and half the pineapple mixture. Repeat the layers. Divide the toasted coconut among the six glasses. Garnish each parfait with a slice of star fruit and a slice of the reserved pineapple, and serve.

NOTE: To toast the coconut, preheat the broiler and spread the coconut on a baking sheet. Toast for 3 minutes, until the coconut turns light brown.

NOTES FROM THE INN:
PUBLICITY

How do you get into a magazine? How do you keep getting featured? The answer is partly prospecting, partly good fortune, and partly consistency. We realized from the beginning that just creating a beautiful inn would not guarantee a successful business. But the renovation and furnishing of the inn left us no funds for marketing expenses, hiring a public relations firm, or sending out large mailings. Any publicity we garnered would have to be a result of the only asset we had at our disposal at the time: our own talents, and of course the inn itself.

Some of the publicity for the inn has resulted from sending information, along with Bob's photographs, to magazines and newspapers. In the early days, I sent out invitations for free overnight stays or complimentary dinners, which helped us get articles in some smaller publications, since they often don't have the budget to send their writers on an overnight trip. Often something to eat accompanied the invitation. (When we had our place in Maine, I sent a live lobster to one editor!) We developed a collection of enthusiastic press clippings, mainly from small magazines and local newspapers, to form the basis of a press kit. One of our favorite early clips was a brief mention in the Gault Millau newsletter, entitled "Skip Church and Eat Instead." Another small but productive piece ran in the *Los Angeles Times*, calling the inn "a couple of acres of bliss." We've often used this simple but powerful phrase as a tag line in our advertising.

Our first major magazine coverage was in a now-defunct periodical called *Country Inns*. We attracted the editor's attention simply by sending some photographs (it's an asset to have a professional photographer "in house") and some handmade pretzels (pretzels are a Pennsylvania Dutch specialty). As a result of that first article, our phone literally did not stop ringing for about six weeks. And we now had a full-color, professionally photographed article for our press kit. Eventually we would be named to the magazine's "Year's Best Inns" list, another nice clip for our kit. We then sent a press kit to *Country Homes* magazine. They had already heard about us from a freelance writer (maybe one of those "free" invitations from early on?), so they arranged to do an article the next year. Sometimes the process takes years, depending on how far ahead the magazines work. Sometimes the article gets bumped for reasons unknown (this happened several times with *Country Inns*). Sometimes you have no idea that someone staying at your inn is actually a writer (*Washingtonian* magazine—another favorite clip: "a romantic spot with wonderful food"). If you're really lucky, someone invites you to cook breakfast on the *Today Show*.

The *Today Show* invitation came as a result of the article in *Country Homes*, somehow through a connection between the publisher and the network. It was my first appearance on national television. The network arranged for Bob and me to stay in a luxury hotel on Central Park the night before. They sent an NBC limo to pick us up on the morning of my appearance. I sat, dressed in my chef's whites, in the "Green Room" next to

James Carville, the Democratic political advisor, and we talked about New Orleans and food. After my segment, in which Katie Couric and I cooked breakfast crepes in about two minutes flat, Bob took some photos of us together. The appearance on the show really didn't generate many reservations at the inn (I think most people tune out by the time they get to the cooking segments), but the photos of Katie and me are real attention-grabbers in the press kit.

The final part of getting publicity is maintaining consistency. Have you ever been drawn to a restaurant or inn whose advertising boasts "Featured in *Bon Appétit*" only to find out the "feature" ran more than ten years ago? The consistent quality of our inn has generated a steady flow of publicity since the first major magazine article appeared in 1991. We've had at least one major feature for each year we've been in business (some years many more). Yes, part of it has been prospecting and part being in the right place at the right time, but overall it's been the consistent quality of our product (the inn and the food) that has made us attractive to major publications. No amount of marketing or public relations expertise can surpass the basic tenet that you should always work to exceed your customers' expectations. You may be able to get an editor's attention once on sheer luck, but to do so repeatedly requires a level of consistency that makes you stand out from the competition. In the end, though, publicity only helps you get the customers' attention; it's up to you to make them happy with their choice and to keep them coming back.

Baked French Toast with Peaches and Blueberries

SERVES 6

Somewhere between traditional French toast and bread pudding, this French toast is baked in individual dishes for an elegant presentation. Fresh summer peaches and blueberries are my favorite accompaniments, but it's so popular that we also serve it with caramelized apples and cranberry sauce in the fall.

Six 1-inch-thick slices Simple Brioche Loaf (page 62) or challah

4 large eggs

¾ cup cream

¼ cup milk

6 tablespoons granulated sugar

6 tablespoons light brown sugar

1 pint blueberries

2 tablespoons fresh lemon juice

2 tablespoons unsalted butter

3 large peaches, peeled, pitted, and sliced

2 tablespoons Grand Marnier or brandy

---

1. Preheat the oven to 350°F. Butter six 3-inch-wide ramekins or soufflé dishes.

2. Cut the brioche into 1-inch cubes. In a large mixing bowl, whisk together the eggs, cream, milk, 2 tablespoons of the granulated sugar, and 2 tablespoons of the brown sugar. Add the brioche cubes and toss to coat evenly. Divide the mixture among the six ramekins.

3. Place the ramekins in a 9 × 13-inch baking pan, and add boiling water until it reaches halfway up the sides of the ramekins. Bake for 15 to 18 minutes, until lightly browned and firm.

4. In the meantime, combine the blueberries, lemon juice, and remaining 4 tablespoons granulated sugar in a small saucepan. Simmer over low heat, stirring often, until syrupy, 3 to 4 minutes. Keep warm.

5. Melt the butter in a medium skillet. Add the peaches and sprinkle the remaining 4 tablespoons brown sugar over them. Sauté until beginning to caramelize, about 3 minutes. Add the Grand Marnier, ignite if desired (remove the skillet from the heat, and standing as far back as possible, ignite the liquid with a long match; swirl the skillet around until the flame dies out), and allow to burn out. Cook for 2 minutes more.

6. Invert the ramekins onto individual plates so the puddings are browned side up. Spoon the warm peaches and blueberry sauce over them, and serve.

Brioche French Toast with Fall Fruit

This is a simple French toast dish made sublime with the addition of a delicious autumnal fruit compote. Mascarpone is soft Italian cream cheese; it's available at specialty stores.

---

3 McIntosh or Rome apples, peeled, cored, and sliced into ½-inch-thick wedges

3 Bosc or Comice pears, peeled, cored, and sliced into ½-inch-thick wedges

¼ cup fresh lemon juice

4 tablespoons unsalted butter

¼ cup light brown sugar

1 vanilla bean, split lengthwise

½ cup dried cranberries

1 cup seedless red grapes

2 tablespoons Grand Marnier or brandy

¼ cup fresh orange juice

½ teaspoon ground allspice

1 recipe Simple Brioche Loaf (page 62) or loaf of challah

6 large eggs

½ cup heavy cream

2 tablespoons corn oil

3 ounces mascarpone

---

1. Toss the apples and pears in a bowl with the lemon juice. Melt 2 tablespoons of the butter in a large skillet over high heat. Add the apples and pears and sauté for 2 minutes. Add the brown sugar, vanilla bean, and dried cranberries, and sauté for 2 minutes. Add the grapes and sauté for 2 to 3 minutes, until they just begin to soften. Add the Grand Marnier, and flame if desired (remove the skillet from the heat, and standing as far back as possible, ignite the liquid with a long match; swirl the skillet around until the flame dies out). Stir in the orange juice and allspice and cook until the mixture thickens slightly, about 2 minutes. Remove the vanilla bean and keep the mixture warm.

2. Preheat the oven to 325°F.

3. Trim the ends of the bread loaf and cut it into twelve slices. Whisk together the eggs and cream in a large bowl. Dip the bread slices into the mixture, coating them evenly, and put them on a plate.

4. Melt the remaining 2 tablespoons butter with the corn oil in a large skillet. When the butter stops foaming, place the bread slices in the skillet, in batches, and cook until browned, 1 to 2 minutes on each side. Place the French toast on a baking sheet, transfer it to the oven, and bake for 5 minutes. Cut the slices in half diagonally, and place four pieces on each of six warmed plates. Top each serving with about 1 tablespoon of the mascarpone. Divide the warm compote among them, and serve.

VARIATION: Add plums to the compote. Stir toasted walnuts or pecans into the warm compote just before serving.

NOTE: The compote may be made up to 24 hours in advance and refrigerated until ready to serve. When ready to serve, rewarm the compote—gently, to avoid making the fruit mushy. The French toast may be made up to 2 hours before the final baking.

You can prevent peeled fruit from browning by immersing it in a bowl filled with cold water acidulated with 1 tablespoon lemon juice or with Fruit Fresh, a flavorless powdered ascorbic acid (vitamin C) that is used in canning.

Simple Brioche Loaf

Freshly baked brioche is often available at bakeries, but because I use brioche in so many dishes, I make this simple version in a loaf pan and slice off what I need.

½ cup milk

1 package active dry yeast

2½ cups all-purpose flour

½ cup unsalted butter, softened

2 tablespoons sugar

1 teaspoon salt

2 large eggs

---

1. Butter an 8½- or 9-inch loaf pan. Line the sides and bottom with parchment paper, and butter again.

2. Heat the milk in a medium-size saucepan over low heat until it is just warm (110° to 115°F). Remove the pan from the heat and pour the milk into a small bowl. Stir in the yeast and 1 cup of the flour. Cover the bowl with plastic wrap and set aside for about 10 minutes.

3. Combine the butter, sugar, salt, and eggs in a food processor or mixer bowl. Add the remaining 1½ cups flour and process until smooth. Add the yeast mixture and process again until smooth. Turn the dough onto a lightly floured surface and knead for about 5 minutes, until smooth and elastic. Shape the dough into a loaf and press it into the prepared pan. Cover the pan and allow the dough to rise until it almost reaches the top, about 1 hour.

4. When the rising is almost complete, preheat the oven to 375°F.

5. Using a sharp knife, make three slash marks across the top of the loaf. Bake for about 40 minutes, until golden.

6. Place the pan on a rack to cool the bread for 5 minutes. Then turn it out of the pan and finish cooling it on its side (alternating sides) until completely cool (this prevents the bread from compressing).

NOTES FROM THE INN:
THE DIFFICULT GUEST

Most of our guests come to the inn to have a good time, but sometimes I have to wonder. We've had only a couple of really challenging guests, but we tend to remember them because there are so few of them. They leave a lasting impression.

Some guests make unusual requests, like the one who asked for a bed with sturdy posts, "strong enough that you might tie something around them." Some guests try to convince us to make exceptions, like the couple who insisted that we should allow their perfectly behaved English mastiff (a rather large breed of dog) to stay with them. They must have assumed they would get a different person if they called back, because they called an hour later to try to book a room "in a separate building with a private entrance." Another couple convinced us that we would never even know their perfectly behaved child was in the building. Later, when it turned out he was less than perfectly behaved and other guests complained, they checked out early and contested their credit card charge with a series of letters making blatantly false allegations. It took us months to resolve the matter and to collect the amount owed. One couple was so exuberant in their affection for each other that it caused our dog, Smokey, to begin howling in the middle of the night.

Our evening turndown service has often allowed us to see a side of our guests that we really wished we hadn't. Although we inform guests of the service, some of them leave rather personal items lying out on the bed. These have included revealing Polaroids (imagine the challenge of serving breakfast to someone who you have just seen in a compromising pose), handcuffs and whips, and in one instance, a carefully laid out array of illegal drugs. One pair of guests even displayed framed photos of themselves with another couple enjoying a champagne toast . . . completely naked. In these cases, we usually tiptoe out of the room without touching a thing.

But these unusual discoveries are minor compared to dealing with difficult guests. One of our most difficult encounters began as soon as the guest arrived. Typically, we take our arriving guests on a brief tour to show them around the inn. While we walk through the guest areas, we mention things that will make their stay more enjoyable, such as what time breakfast is served, where the afternoon tea will be set out, and where they can find complimentary beverages any time of day. We point out the tour books about the area, the folder with restaurant menus, and the office door marked "Private" where they can find us when we're not at the front desk. The entire tour takes about two minutes. Most people are very congenial and interested, but on one rare occasion, a guest informed me that she could not tolerate such trivia. With courteous restraint, I immediately took her up to her room and hoped I'd seen the last of her. Later that day, I went into the restaurant kitchen to begin baking for afternoon tea and found this same guest at my range—cooking! Apparently she had decided to make herself something to eat.

Another memorable guest spent some time earlier in the day bragging to Bob about how he could get complimentary stays and meals at the casinos in Atlantic City by lodging bogus complaints. After an evening of drinking, he must have forgotten this conversation. At dinner, he ate his entire entree (a veal chop with chanterelle mushrooms) and then called Bob over to say that he had "found something" in his dinner. Bob whisked the plate into the kitchen (where he and I were the only ones working) and we were astounded—it was a cigarette butt. Of course neither of us smoke, so we strongly suspected the guest had placed it on the plate. Somehow this guest must have assumed we had a larger staff and was hoping to pin the evil deed on a prep cook or dishwasher, and receive a complimentary weekend. The weirdest part was that we didn't know what to say, so Bob diplomatically told him it was just a mushroom stem. The guest became so sheepish and incredibly complimentary about the meal that we knew he was guilty. We even wondered if we'd deprived him of his "lucky cigarette butt." When I later saw a news story about a man who was arrested at the casinos for falsely claiming he'd found cigarette butts in his food, I couldn't help wondering if this was our guest.

We feel fortunate that we don't get more problematic guests, given the unique nature of innkeeping. The idea of welcoming complete strangers into your home doesn't seem to fit into modern times. Of course that's the appeal of staying at an inn—it's a pleasure to be personally welcomed into a beautiful and comfortable environment. The world we create for our guests allows them to safely step away from the risks and stress of modern living, if only for a few days. The downside is that we sometimes risk allowing questionable people into this world. The upside for us is that most of our guests are here simply to enjoy themselves—and the majority leave their handcuffs at home.

Setting an Elegant Table

I've always thought that breakfast is an obvious but little-used opportunity for entertaining. Everyone seems to enjoy being served a special breakfast, but there are few chances to partake of it in a refined setting. We make our breakfast service elegant every day of the week. An important part of doing so is the care we take in setting the table.

First, we arrange the fine linens, bone china, and silver place settings on the tables well before serving time. Fresh flowers grace the tables. Classical music plays softly in the background. We light the candles on each table, and guests are seated as they arrive. We serve our fresh fruit juices and breakfast drinks in crystal champagne flutes. The overall mood is one of relaxed elegance. Although guests often expect this ambience for dinner, they are pleasantly surprised to be treated to it at breakfast.

Take advantage of a holiday or special occasion to make your own breakfast memorable by setting an elegant table. Whether you're setting a romantic table for two or planning a larger gathering for family or friends, you'll be amazed at how much the extra attention adds to even the simplest meal.

What Kind of Inn Am I?

There are many different types and sizes of country inns. There are professionally decorated inns. There are inns with bellboys and valet parking attendants. There are inns with general managers and owners that you'll never meet. I've stayed at inns like these and found many of them to be wonderful. But our inn is not like that.

Our inn is very much about us, but not literally. It's easy for the owners of a small inn to allow themselves to become the focus of attention or even to allow their hired chef to become that focal point (for example, when the chef is the owner, as in so many wonderful European inns and some of the best American ones). Some inns even go to great expense to promote their properties through a personal focal point. I've always found it to be a bad idea. For one thing, what if the chef leaves and takes your reputation with him or her? What if the innkeeper who's supposed to be mingling with guests during evening wine and cheese is feeling under the weather? This approach requires the innkeeper (and in some cases the chef) to be present all the time; otherwise, guests may rightfully feel they've received less than they were promised. On the other hand, we *are* here all the time, but we don't like that to be obvious. We like to think that we're available when our guests need us and invisible when they don't.

It's sometimes a delicate balance. We want to be friendly and welcoming to our guests, but we don't want to be intrusive. We know our guests are at the inn for their own personal enjoyment and not to be with us. This is not the Bob and Donna Show—we're not the "talent." We're more like good producers; we put together all the important elements to provide the best setting possible for our guests and then allow them to enjoy it.

We've tried to accomplish this combination of cordiality and professionalism in a number of ways. We have separate living quarters but we still live in the building, so we're almost always accessible to guests. We've created a decor that's warm and comfortable, without making guests feel as though they're staying in "our house." None of our personal effects are in the inn—no family photos, no pets, not even grandma's antique desk (if we had such a thing!). Separate seating arrangements in the dining rooms and common areas neither force social interactions nor preclude them. Our first brochure advertised our inn as having "the warmth of a country bed and breakfast with the elegant amenities of a full-service inn." This is the balance we've worked to achieve through the years, although depending on the circumstances and the needs of the guests, it sometimes swings to one side or the other.

This is the type of inn we run. But it doesn't have to be the type of inn *you* run or fantasize about running. That's one of the great features of country inns—they're all as unique as the people who dream them up.

Apricot Almond French Toast

SERVES 6

Apricot preserves are one of my favorite prepared items to incorporate into a breakfast dish. They add an elegant glaze to many baked goods and are especially tasty when paired with almonds in this easy French toast.

6 large eggs	2 tablespoons corn oil
½ cup heavy cream	2 cups apricot preserves
½ teaspoon almond extract	¼ cup Amaretto or brandy
12 slices French bread	½ cup sliced almonds
2 tablespoons unsalted butter	4 ounces mascarpone

1. Preheat the oven to 375°F.

2. Whisk the eggs, cream, and almond extract together in a medium bowl. Dip each piece of bread into the egg mixture, coating both sides.

3. Heat the butter and corn oil in a large skillet until the butter is melted and foamy. Add the bread slices, in batches, and sauté each side over medium heat until golden brown, about 2 minutes per side. Place the bread slices flat on a baking sheet.

4. Mix the preserves and Amaretto in a small saucepan and bring just to a boil. Remove the mixture from the heat and spoon it evenly over the bread slices. Sprinkle the almonds evenly over the bread slices. Bake for 4 to 6 minutes, until the almonds are just toasted. Tuck a teaspoon of mascarpone between two warm overlapping slices on each plate, and serve.

NOTE: This is an excellent dish for a buffet brunch since it can be prepared up to 2 hours ahead and then glazed just before serving. Although it will yield a different flavor, you can substitute softened cream cheese for the mascarpone.

Apple Cinnamon Stuffed French Toast

SERVES 6

Stuffed French toast is one of my most requested breakfast dishes, so I'm constantly thinking up new combinations to offer our returning guests. We serve this lightly sweetened filling of apples, sour cream, and cream cheese encased in freshly baked cinnamon bread, but French bread may be substituted if you can't find unsliced cinnamon loaves. Melted apple jelly gives the dish a finishing glaze.

---

8 ounces cream cheese, softened

¼ cup sour cream

2 tablespoons sugar

1 teaspoon ground cinnamon

2 apples, peeled, cored, and finely chopped

Six 2-inch-thick slices cinnamon bread

3 large eggs

¼ cup heavy cream

2 tablespoons unsalted butter

2 tablespoons corn oil

½ cup apple jelly

---

1. Preheat the oven to 375°F. Lightly grease a baking sheet with solid vegetable shortening.

2. Combine the cream cheese, sour cream, sugar, and cinnamon in a mixing bowl and beat with an electric mixer until smooth. Fold in the chopped apple.

3. Slice a 2-inch-wide opening into the center of the top of each piece of bread, cutting down almost all the way to the bottom. Spoon about 2 tablespoons of the cream cheese mixture into each pocket.

4. Whisk together the eggs and cream in a small mixing bowl. Dip each slice of French toast into the egg mixture, coating each side evenly.

5. Heat the butter and corn oil in a large skillet until the butter is melted and foamy. Sauté the bread pieces until golden on both sides, about 1 to 2 minutes per side. Place the sautéed pieces on the prepared baking sheet, transfer to the oven, and bake for 10 minutes, until the filling is heated through.

6. In the meantime, heat the apple jelly in a small saucepan or in the microwave until melted. Brush the tops of the baked French toast with the glaze, and serve.

Orange Crepes with Strawberry-Rhubarb Glaze

SERVES 6

Perhaps, like me, you've seen the reddish green stalks of rhubarb at a market or farm stand and were a little unsure about how to prepare them. Since it's so widely available in our area in early summer, I decided to conquer my fear of rhubarb and set about incorporating it into breakfast and dinner entrees. One of my favorite versions is this strawberry-rhubarb glaze. The rhubarb is first softened in an orange sugar syrup, then stirred into the strawberries to add a slightly tart complexity to the finished syrup. The syrup may also be made with just the oranges, but you'll miss out on the interesting tangy flavor that the rhubarb imparts.

---

4 ounces cream cheese	½ cup light corn syrup
1 cup sugar	2 oranges, peeled and cut into
1 teaspoon orange extract	¼-inch wedges
1¼ cups ricotta cheese	3 stalks fresh rhubarb, trimmed
¾ cup all-purpose flour	and cut into 1-inch pieces
1 tablespoon grated orange zest	2 tablespoons unsalted butter
1 large egg	2 cups hulled and halved
1 large egg yolk	strawberries
¾ cup half-and-half	¼ cup Grand Marnier
½ cup fresh orange juice	

---

1. With an electric mixer, beat the cream cheese, 3 tablespoons of the sugar, and the orange extract in a medium bowl until smooth. Stir in the ricotta until just combined. Set the filling aside.

2. Combine the flour, 2 tablespoons of the sugar, and the orange zest in a large mixing bowl. In a smaller bowl, whisk together the egg, egg yolk, half-and-half, and ¼ cup water. Pour the wet ingredients into the dry ingredients and stir until just combined.

3. Lightly butter a 9- or 10-inch crepe pan or skillet (or use nonstick cooking spray), and heat it over medium heat until hot but not smoking. Ladle in about 2 tablespoons of the batter, tilting the pan to evenly coat the bottom. Cook until the edges just begin to curl and brown, 1 to 2 minutes. Then flip and cook the other side for 1 minute. Continue until six crepes are completed. Cover and set aside.

4. Heat the orange juice, corn syrup, and ½ cup of the sugar in a medium-size saucepan until the sugar is dissolved. Stir in the orange wedges and rhubarb. Bring just to a boil, then reduce the heat to a simmer and cook until the mixture is thick and syrupy, about 10 minutes. Keep warm.

5. Preheat the oven to 375°F.

6. Place 2 tablespoons of the reserved filling in the center of each crepe, and fold up the bottom third of the crepe. Fold the two sides in, then continue rolling from the bottom until you have a neat rectangular package. Place the crepes on a lightly greased baking sheet. Bake for 8 minutes, until just heated through.

7. In the meantime, melt the butter in a medium skillet. Add the strawberries and cook for 1 minute on high heat. Sprinkle with the remaining 3 tablespoons sugar, and continue cooking and stirring until the strawberries begin to release a little juice, about 2 minutes. Add the Grand Marnier, and flame if desired (remove the skillet from the heat, and standing as far back as possible, ignite the liquid with a long match; swirl the skillet around until the flame dies out). Add the orange rhubarb syrup and cook for 1 minute longer. Place a crepe on each plate, top with the glaze, and serve.

NOTE: Crepes may be made up to 24 hours in advance, stacked with waxed paper, and stored in an airtight container. The filling may be made up to 24 hours in advance and refrigerated until ready to use. The syrup is best made just before serving, to preserve the fresh flavor of the rhubarb.

One Batch at a Time

Once we started harvesting our own berries, I wanted to try making jams for the inn. All of my knowledgeable jam-making friends warned me off, saying it's a waste of time to make small batches of jams or preserves. It's too much work for just a few jars, they cautioned—and it's better to make a lot at once, since you can always give away the extra jars as gifts.

I actually prefer making a few jars at a time for a number of reasons. I get to use my own berries when they're just picked. I get to play around a little with different textures and recipes. I can also take a small amount of fruit and make a few jars of refrigerator (unsealed) jam for our immediate enjoyment. We always seem to have plenty. When you think of it, how many jars of preserves can you really use, anyway? Our three black currant plants yield enough preserves to last into the winter months, making the perfect accompaniment for an array of roasted game dishes.

So if you've ever been overwhelmed at the idea of making your own jam but still would like to try it, follow my advice and start out in small batches. It's very satisfying and it doesn't take a lot of time. All of you knowledgeable canners, though, please disregard my advice. Those of us who've received your homemade jams as gifts prefer that you continue making your wonderful large batches to share with us!

Baked Pancakes with Berries and Mascarpone

SERVES 6

This is a great way to serve pancakes without having to hover over the griddle. The pancakes are baked simultaneously and then transferred from the pans to warmed plates. Individual tart pans with removable bottoms make it easy to remove the pancakes. The fresh berry sauce is a sweet finish for the almond-scented pancakes.

---

5 tablespoons unsalted butter	1 cup strawberries, hulled and
1¼ cups all-purpose flour	quartered
1¼ teaspoons baking powder	½ cup sugar
½ teaspoon baking soda	2 tablespoons brandy
½ teaspoon salt	½ cup raspberries
1 cup half-and-half	½ cup blackberries
1 teaspoon almond extract	3 ounces mascarpone
5 large eggs, separated	

---

1. Preheat the oven to 400°F. Butter six individual tart pans with removable bottoms.

2. Melt 3 tablespoons of the butter in a saucepan and allow to cool slightly.

3. Combine the flour, baking powder, baking soda, and salt in a large mixing bowl. In another bowl, whisk together the half-and-half, almond extract, and egg yolks. In a third bowl, beat the egg whites until they form stiff peaks.

4. Stir the half-and-half mixture into the dry ingredients. Stir in the melted butter. Then fold in the egg whites. Place the prepared tart pans on a baking sheet, and ladle the mixture into them. Bake for 12 to 15 minutes, until puffed and lightly browned.

5. In the meantime, melt the remaining 2 tablespoons butter in a large skillet. Add the strawberries and cook for 1 minute on high heat. Sprinkle with the sugar and continue cooking and stirring until the strawberries begin to release a little juice, about 2 minutes. Add the brandy, and flame if desired (remove the skillet from the heat, and standing as far back as possible, ignite the liquid with a long match; swirl the skillet around until the flame dies out). Add the raspberries and blackberries, and cook 1 minute longer.

6. Unmold the pancakes onto individual plates. Place about a tablespoon of mascarpone on top of each pancake. Spoon the berry sauce over the top, and serve.

About Cancellation Policies

All lodging facilities have a deadline for canceling a reservation, beyond which you will not receive a refund. Large hotels often allow you to cancel up to six P.M. on the day of your reservation, but smaller properties need to be strict because losing a single reservation represents a significant loss of income. For example, if a 400-room hotel loses a reservation, that's 1/400 of their possible revenue, or 0.25 percent. If an eight-room inn loses a reservation, it's ⅛ of their potential income, or 12.5 percent. If it's a reservation for several nights, you can understand that this represents a considerable loss for a small property like ours.

Running a small inn means that you need a cancellation policy that is fair to guests but prevents those rooms from staying vacant. As an innkeeper, you must be clear about the policy at the time the reservation is made. We base the length of time needed to receive a refund on how likely it is that we will be able to fill the room. With at least two weeks' notice, there is a fairly good chance that we can rerent the room (we're not always successful). Since people book further ahead on holiday weekends or at certain peak seasons of the year, we require longer notice for these special times. But even with this policy, we still retain only the deposit, which is often a fraction of the total amount lost.

We're reasonable people, so when there are extreme circumstances, we relax our policy. When a guest needs to cancel because a close family member has died or has been diagnosed with a serious or fatal disease, we make an exception. The problem is that this excuse for canceling has been used so often that we've grown a little suspicious over the years. When someone has a legitimate problem, they're often so grief-stricken that they don't even care about the deposit and they're being courteous by calling to let us know. On the other hand, some people seem so concerned with getting a refund that it's hard to believe they have a legitimate personal crisis. We now ask for some kind of written confirmation of the problem, as airlines do if a flight reservation must be canceled due to an emergency.

It's unfortunate that a small number of people have such disregard for business owners, especially for those with smaller inns or restaurants. When you own a small business, this careless attitude can mean the difference between paying your bills and not paying them. The good thing is that most of the people who book reservations with us respect our cancellation policy and understand the implications for us. But when people are not understanding, I try to be considerate when they get belligerent about it, especially when they claim they were never notified. I know they were notified several different ways and that I have all the documentation I'll need to prove it. After having a few really nasty people yell at me over the phone, I must confess that I'm often secretly glad they had to cancel anyway.

Apple and Walnut Pancakes

This tasty version of old-fashioned pancakes is easy to make since the apples and walnuts are folded into the batter. Warm some real maple syrup before serving.

---

1 cup all-purpose flour	¼ cup unsalted butter, melted
2 tablespoons sugar	3 apples, peeled, cored, and
4 teaspoons baking powder	coarsely chopped
½ teaspoon salt	½ cup walnuts, coarsely chopped
1 cup sour cream	Whipped butter
6 large eggs, separated	Maple syrup

---

1. Combine the flour, sugar, baking powder, and salt in the bowl of an electric mixer. Beat in the sour cream until smooth. Beat in the egg yolks and melted butter until smooth.

2. In another bowl, whisk the egg whites until soft peaks form. Fold the egg whites into the batter. Fold the apples and walnuts into the batter.

3. Heat a lightly buttered griddle or skillet over medium-high heat, and ladle on the batter to form 3- to 4-inch pancakes. Cook until small bubbles form and edges begin to brown, 2 to 3 minutes. Flip and cook on the other side for 1 to 2 minutes, until just cooked through. Repeat until twelve pancakes are completed.

4. Serve with whipped butter and warm maple syrup.

SOUPS

Soups have always been an important part of our menus and are among our most requested recipes. Some of our soups capture the essence of the season, while others are enjoyable year-round. Soups are among the most versatile dishes you can prepare. They can be the elegant beginning to a formal dinner or they can be shared informally around the kitchen table. They can be part of a multicourse menu or they can be paired with a salad and some crusty bread for an easy weeknight meal.

We offer an array of soups for different meals and seasons. Our fruit soups most often appear on breakfast menus or as a light, refreshing dessert at the end of a warm-weather dinner. Our heartier soups, such as the chowders, are a welcome warm-up in the winter months. Our smooth soups concentrate seasonal ingredients in each creamy spoonful. These soup recipes offer a wide range of styles perfect for family meals as well as entertaining.

Spiced Cranberry Pear Soup

SERVES 6

Fruit soups are usually served chilled and are thought of as summer fare, but here's a warm one to get you through the cold weather.

1 bottle dry red wine	6 pears, peeled and left whole
1 star anise	2 cups fresh cranberries
1 cinnamon stick	½ cup fresh orange juice
2 whole cloves	½ teaspoon ground nutmeg
¼ cup sugar	Grated orange zest, for garnish

1. Combine the wine, star anise, cinnamon stick, cloves, and sugar in a saucepan that is just large enough to hold the pears. Bring the liquid to a boil and add the pears, stems up. Simmer for 15 to 20 minutes, until the pears are tender. Remove the pears. Discard the star anise and cinnamon stick, and bring the poaching liquid to a rapid boil. Add the cranberries and cook until they pop, about 5 minutes. Allow the mixture to cool.

2. Remove the stems from the pears and cut the pears into chunks. Combine the pears, poaching liquid with cranberries, orange juice, and nutmeg in a food processor or blender, and process until smooth. Strain the mixture into a saucepan and heat it gently. Sprinkle each serving with orange zest.

NOTE: This soup may be made up to 24 hours in advance and stored, covered, in the refrigerator.

Apricot Raspberry Soup

SERVES 6

Red raspberries give this chilled soup a pink hue. The yogurt adds tang and a creamy finish to the sweet flavor of the apricots.

1 pint red raspberries	12 apricots, peeled and pitted
¼ cup sugar	1½ cups apricot nectar
2 tablespoons fresh lemon juice	½ cup low-fat yogurt

Combine the raspberries, sugar, and lemon juice in a food processor or blender, and process until smooth. Press the puree through a sieve to remove the seeds. Combine half of the raspberry puree with the apricots and apricot nectar in a food processor or blender, and process until smooth. Add the yogurt and process until just combined. Spoon the soup into chilled bowls, swirl in the remaining raspberry puree, and serve.

NOTE: The raspberry puree may be made up to 24 hours in advance and refrigerated until you are ready to make the soup. Blend it with the apricots just before serving.

A Demitasse of Soup

I love tasting unique soups when we dine out, but I'm seldom able to finish both soup and an appetizer. When ordering à la carte, I usually end up passing on the soup and having an appetizer instead. At the inn, I've found a way to allow customers to taste one of our delicious soups and still feel comfortable finishing the rest of their meal as well. Our complimentary first course is most often a tiny cup of soup, served in an espresso or demitasse cup. I serve only smooth soups so that guests may simply pick up the cup and sip it, instead of having to use a spoon. It's a great way to allow guests a little sampling without serving an entire course. Some guests enjoy the soup so much that they ask for a bowl of it.

Cantaloupe Orange Soup

SERVES 6

We serve this chilled soup as a fruit course for breakfast during the height of the summer, when our home-grown melons are at their sweetest and most plentiful. With the simple addition of a scoop of Orange Champagne Granita (page 216), this soup becomes an elegant summer-time dessert.

---

2 medium cantaloupes, or 3 small Charentais melons, halved and seeded

1 cup fresh orange juice

Sugar to taste

3 oranges

Fresh mint sprigs

---

1. Remove the rind from the cantaloupes and cut the fruit into chunks. Combine the cantaloupe and orange juice in a food processor or blender, and process until smooth. Add sugar to taste, and process until combined.

2. Cut the oranges in half. Remove just the fruit from the oranges (the way you would cut the segments from a grapefruit, leaving the skin behind).

3. Divide the soup among six chilled bowls. Divide the orange pieces among the bowls, and garnish with the mint sprigs. Serve immediately.

NOTE: This chilled soup may be made up to 2 hours in advance but will need to be blended again just before serving. I prefer to use a blender rather than a food processor because it provides more aeration, resulting in a lighter consistency.

In Search of the Perfect Melon

Several times a year we take the opportunity to close the inn and go on vacation, in an effort to free ourselves of the day-to-day responsibilities of innkeeping. But somehow the inn is always traveling along with us. One of our favorite things is to visit gardens, since we're always looking for new designs and plants to add to our ever-expanding landscaping repertoire. Several summers ago, while staying in the Vaucluse region of southern France, we happened upon a wonderful market in the town of Cavaillon, just southeast of Avignon. If we had not driven into the market area by chance, surely we would have been able to find it by the aroma, alluringly sweet, of melon. Several of the stands were heaped with melons unlike any we had ever seen. About the size of softballs, they had a smooth golden exterior with deep green stripes. The flesh was orange, juicy, and fragrant. We were offered a taste, and the sweet flavor exploded in our mouths. We had always relied on our local farmers to supply us with the best and sweetest melons, but now we decided to bring the seeds home with us and grow these melons ourselves, at the inn.

We bought several melons and sliced into them, carefully reserving the seeds. My grandmother had grown up on a farm in New Jersey, and she had showed me as a child how to dry seeds for the next year's garden. The only problem was that up until this time, we had grown only flowers and herbs in our gardens. And so began our foray into the world of vegetable and fruit gardening. We now grow a wide range of fruits and vegetables, including, of course, the melons. In the winter months, we are inundated with catalogs from seed companies and nurseries—who now, it seems, have also discovered the secret of the perfect melon. Sometimes called Cavaillon after the region in France in which we first discovered them, the seeds are available from Shepherd's Garden and other seed catalogs under their more common name, Charentais. But if you don't have an inclination to grow your own, you'll now find them in the Cantaloupe Orange Soup at the Inn at Twin Linden.

Sparkling Strawberry Soup

Tea is the secret ingredient that gives this soup its interesting flavor. Macerating the strawberries in sugar causes them to soften and release their juices.

2 quarts strawberries	1 cup orange juice
¼ cup sugar	1 split of champagne (187 ml), or
1 cup iced tea	12 ounces club soda

1. Reserve 6 strawberries for garnish. Remove the hulls from the remaining strawberries and cut them into quarters. Toss the strawberries with the sugar in a large bowl, and set aside for 15 minutes.

2. Combine the macerated strawberries, iced tea, and orange juice in a food processor or blender, and process until smooth. Stir in the champagne.

3. Divide the soup among six chilled bowls. Slice each of the reserved whole strawberries up to the hull, and fan the slices out. Place one strawberry fan in the center of each bowl, and serve.

NOTES FROM THE INN:
THE CAVE

We live in the back part of the inn, in an area we used to not-so-affectionately refer to as "the cave." Since initially we spent any profits on making improvements to the inn, our quarters remained in the original "basic" condition (a kind word) that they had been in when we bought the property. Even a fresh coat of paint didn't help. Our living space consisted of a series of tiny rooms, making it difficult for us to see how to get started. Everything seemed to hinge on something else. We couldn't work on the kitchen until we first redid the bathroom. We couldn't redo the bathroom until we added another bathroom upstairs. We couldn't add another bathroom until we reconfigured a guest room that was next to our bedroom on the second floor.

So we waited. One fateful weekend, Bob invited some of our best customers into the cave to look at a videotape of one of my television appearances. I was horrified. The next day I called my contractor. We had lived in the cave long enough.

Since the cave was our only place to hang out when not with guests, the project was quite a disruption. I didn't mind, because I was so excited at the prospect of having new quarters, but the inconvenience made Bob and my dog, Smokey, very grumpy. First we had to clear out the old furniture and kitchen fixtures. I wasn't sure either Bob or Smokey would ever forgive me when I sold their favorite television-watching couch. I was so happy to sell the old kitchen cabinets that I threw in the countertops, sinks, and even the dishwasher as a bonus. Suddenly there was no place to watch TV or to eat dinner! While the first floor of the cave was being torn out, the only clean area was our tiny bedroom. Bob grumbled about missing his old sofa. Smokey broke out in hives.

Our contractors tore out plaster to create a vaulted ceiling and added windows so that we might enjoy the garden view. We removed the wall between the kitchen and the old TV room to create an open "great room" effect. Even finding an abandoned brick chimney in the walls didn't stop progress. As the contractors installed the new recessed lighting, I chiseled out bricks one at a time, then gleefully swung a sledgehammer until the entire chimney was removed. While working on the inn had been rewarding for me, this project had the added motivation of creating a new kitchen for my personal use. We could entertain again. I would find a new couch that would be aesthetically pleasing as well as comfortable. I would admire the blazing fire in the raised hearth while I prepared dinner for family and friends. We would have a home within our home.

Part of my overall design was to make our living quarters look vastly different from the inn. I wanted to walk through our office door marked "Private" and into a completely different world. The first thing I decided was that the kitchen area should be warm and welcoming—and virtually free of stainless steel. My professional kitchen is an effective work area, but it is just that: a work area. I wanted my home kitchen to represent the nonwork aspects of cooking and to be a pleasant environment for entertaining. Whenever I write recipes for home use, I've found it helpful to test them out on nonprofessional appliances. So I decided not to purchase commercial appliances for my kitchen. Once the construction was complete, contemporary furnishings and black granite countertops would be the finishing touches on our new living space.

Now we relax in our comfortable, elegant great room and are amazed at the transformation that took place. In the cooler months, I enjoy the warm glow of a wood fire while I work on recipes or prepare a holiday dinner. In warmer weather, brilliant blue lobelia and fragrant nasturtiums spill out of hayracks hung just outside our windows. We've added a second-floor master bathroom and renovated the downstairs bath, with black marble and white cabinets. The days of the cave are gone, and I can't say I miss them. I never really liked that old sofa anyway. Watching him relax by the fire with our dogs, I get the feeling that Bob doesn't miss it one bit either.

Peach and Red Wine Soup

SERVES 6

My Italian grandfather used to pour a little of his homemade wine over a freshly sliced peach to enjoy after lunch. As a child, I thought this was a terrible thing to do to a sweet, delicious peach. I've since discovered what a tasty combination it is, especially with the addition of cinnamon and a hint of lemon.

1 bottle red wine	2 teaspoons grated lemon zest
¼ cup packed light brown sugar	3 peaches
1 cinnamon stick	2 tablespoons fresh lemon juice
2 black peppercorns	

1. Combine the wine, brown sugar, cinnamon stick, peppercorns, and lemon zest in a medium saucepan and bring to a boil. Reduce the heat and simmer until reduced by one third, about 10 minutes. Refrigerate for at least 3 hours, until chilled.

2. Just before serving, peel and pit the peaches. Slice the peaches into thin wedges and toss with the lemon juice. Divide the peach slices among six chilled bowls. Strain the red wine mixture through a sieve, and pour it evenly over the peach. Serve.

Chilled Asparagus Soup

SERVES 6

Asparagus blended with leeks and potato makes a tasty spring soup. Stirring in the heavy cream will add a richer flavor, but the soup is perfectly delicious without it. Using white pepper instead of black adds seasoning without marring the soup's beautiful appearance. I like to use a handheld immersion blender on smooth soups just before serving—it lightens the texture and creates a slightly frothy effect.

---

2 pounds asparagus

¼ cup unsalted butter

2 leeks, white part only, thoroughly
washed and coarsely chopped

1 small potato, peeled and diced

2 sprigs flat-leaf parsley

6 cups Basic Chicken Stock
(page 87)

1 teaspoon white pepper

Salt to taste

½ cup heavy cream (optional)

12 chives, chopped

---

1. Trim the woody ends off the asparagus and discard. Bring a small pot of lightly salted water to a boil. Cut off the tips of the asparagus and cook them in the boiling water until they just turn green, about 2 minutes. Immediately drain the tips and submerge them in a bowl of ice water. Reserve 18 tips for the garnish; refrigerate them until ready to serve. Chop the remaining asparagus spears into 1-inch segments.

2. Heat the butter in a large saucepan. Add the leeks and cook until softened, 5 to 7 minutes. Add the potato, parsley, chicken stock, and white pepper, and bring to a boil. Add the asparagus segments and boil at high heat until tender, 5 to 7 minutes. Puree the mixture in batches in a food processor or blender until smooth. Season with salt to taste.

3. Place the mixture in a bowl and set it in a larger bowl filled with ice water; this will cool it rapidly and preserve its bright green color. Stir in the cream if desired, cover, and refrigerate until thoroughly chilled, about 1 hour.

4. Divide the soup among six chilled bowls, and garnish with the reserved tips and the chopped chives.

NOTE: The soup may be made up to 24 hours in advance and refrigerated. Blend the soup again just before serving.

Crab Gazpacho

This version of gazpacho retains the texture of the individual ingredients but allows the flavors to meld together for several hours before it's served. Add the croutons just before serving. I extract my own tomato juice from sweet summer tomatoes for the freshest flavor, but canned tomato juice may also be used.

12 plum tomatoes, seeded and finely chopped

6 scallions, white part only, finely chopped

2 cucumbers, peeled and finely chopped

1 green bell pepper, seeded and finely chopped

1 jalapeño pepper, seeded and finely minced

3 tablespoons extra virgin olive oil

2 tablespoons fresh lemon juice

2½ cups fresh tomato juice

3 tablespoons finely chopped cilantro

2 tablespoons finely chopped flat-leaf parsley

1 teaspoon minced roasted garlic (see Note, page 90)

¼ teaspoon cayenne pepper

¼ teaspoon black pepper

½ teaspoon Old Bay seasoning

Salt to taste

1 pound cooked lump or backfin crabmeat

3 slices French baguette, cut into cubes and toasted

Combine all the ingredients except the crabmeat and the baguette cubes in a large bowl. Fold in the crabmeat. Cover and chill thoroughly, at least 2 hours. Divide the mixture among six chilled bowls. Scatter the croutons over the soup, and serve.

Lobster Thyme Bisque

This is a shortcut version of lobster bisque that is flavored with lobster meat instead of just the shells. At the inn, we freeze any leftover lobster to use in this bisque, which has always been our most popular dinner soup.

---

1 cup unsalted butter	4 plum tomatoes, seeded and
3 celery stalks, coarsely chopped	quartered
2 carrots, peeled and coarsely	3 cups Simple Fish or Basic
chopped	Chicken Stock (pages 88, 87)
1 small onion, peeled and	10 sprigs thyme
quartered, plus ¼ cup finely	2 cups chopped Maine lobster meat
chopped onion	¼ cup all-purpose flour
	2 cups half-and-half

---

1. Melt ½ cup of the butter in a large saucepan. Add the celery, carrots, and quartered onion and cook over medium heat until the vegetables are soft, 8 to 10 minutes. Add the tomatoes and cook for 1 minute. Add the stock, 4 thyme sprigs, lobster, and 2 cups water. Bring the mixture to a boil, then lower the heat to a simmer. Simmer for about 1 hour, until the lobster is falling apart and the liquid is reduced by two thirds.

2. Set a food mill over a bowl, and pour the mixture through it. Crush the vegetables and the lobster in the food mill to extract any juices. Discard the vegetables and lobster meat.

3. In a medium saucepan, melt the remaining ½ cup butter over medium heat. Add the finely chopped onion and cook until translucent, about 2 minutes. Whisk in the flour and cook for 1 minute. Add the lobster stock and bring just to a boil, stirring constantly. Add the half-and-half and bring just to a boil. Serve, garnished with the remaining thyme sprigs.

NOTE: If you don't have a food mill, pour the mixture through a fine-mesh strainer and use the back of a spoon to extract the juices. The soup may be made up to 24 hours in advance, refrigerated, and reheated just before serving.

Basic Chicken Stock

MAKES 2 QUARTS

4 pounds chicken parts	3 thyme sprigs
6 flat-leaf parsley sprigs	1 small onion, quartered
1 bay leaf	1 carrot, chopped

1. Put all the ingredients into a large stockpot, add 4 quarts water, and bring to a boil. Then reduce the heat and simmer for 2½ hours, occasionally skimming off any fat or impurities that rise to the surface.

2. Pour the stock through a colander set over a large pot or bowl, and discard the solids. Let the stock cool slightly, and remove any fat from the surface. If you are not using it right away, store the stock for up to 3 days in the refrigerator or for up to 2 months in the freezer.

Simple Fish Stock

5 pounds fish trimmings from
    white, non-oily fish such as
    flounder, rockfish, and/or
    monkfish
1 leek, thoroughly washed and
    coarsely chopped
1 celery stalk, coarsely chopped

1 carrot, coarsely chopped
1 clove garlic, peeled
1 bay leaf
3 sprigs flat-leaf parsley
3 sprigs thyme
4 black peppercorns
1 bottle dry white wine

1. Put all the ingredients in a large stockpot, add 4 quarts water, and bring to a boil. Reduce the heat and simmer for 2 hours, skimming off any impurities as necessary.

2. Strain the stock through a fine-mesh sieve set over a bowl. The stock may be stored in the refrigerator for up to 2 days or in the freezer for up to 3 months.

NOTES FROM THE INN: THE RESTAURANT

Our restaurant began with the enthusiasm that comes from having no idea what you're getting into. Although the restaurant was part of my country inn fantasy from the beginning, running it is the most intense, pressure-filled job I've ever had. It even causes me to have nightmares. In one of my worst recurring nightmares, it's 5:45 P.M., we're getting ready to seat the first dinner guests, and I suddenly realize I've forgotten to order any food!

Our initial plan was to serve dinner three or four days a week. I would be the chef and Bob would run the front of the house. We hired a high-school girl as a waitress and her friend as a dishwasher. Neither had any experience, which turned out to be good, or they would have quit after the first week. The early days were pure mayhem. I remember nights when the dirty dishes were literally stacked on the floor. I remember people lined up waiting for tables. I remember running out of menu items, and once getting down to only one selection for dessert. I remember being so backed up in the kitchen that I wanted to cry. When I look back on those times, it's amazing how understanding our first customers were.

What kept them coming back was the food. Our local restaurant clientele are mainly transplants from nearby Philadelphia, who appreciate our thoughtful, well-prepared food. They also appreciate a bargain, and our prices were ridiculously low during our early "learning" period. Many of our customers are wine collectors, so our "BYOB" policy was an added attraction. We tried to make up for our mistakes by offering complimentary courses, glasses of champagne, or anything else that allowed our customers to leave satisfied. Finally, Bob became the ultimate "shmoozer," distracting waiting guests with embellished versions of his life story when it seemed their tables would never be ready.

After that first year, we actually started getting good at it. We learned not to overbook tables. We hired experienced waitresses and a dedicated dishwashing crew. I learned how to plan menus and how much food to order each week. As our reputation grew, we expanded the seating in the dining room so that everyone had a view of the gardens. We added a fireplace for cool winter nights and outdoor seating for warm summer evenings. We refined our service. Each night, I prepared an entirely different menu. Our reviews were stellar and our waiting list grew. We became a successful restaurant.

The only problem was, we didn't want to be a restaurant—we wanted to be a country inn. The enthusiasm of our outside diners began to conflict with our vision of a relaxed and soothing atmosphere for our overnight guests. Diners who had waited for tables in the guests' common areas in the early days now wanted to arrive early and enjoy some wine there before dinner. Our staff had grown and was becoming unmanageable. After we closed up around midnight, Bob and I would lie in bed, wide-eyed and sleepless, rehashing the night's events, discussing staff problems, and bemoaning supplier glitches. We wondered what we'd do if I actually got sick one night and we had no chef. We started dreading the weekend and fantasized about selling.

So we did something dramatic: We closed the restaurant. We decided to refocus our efforts on our overnight guests by limiting our outside clientele. We would still offer dinner to the public, but on a very limited basis. I needed to reinvent our dinner service and to renew my enthusiasm as a chef.

We reopened the restaurant with a multi-course fixed menu dinner, in the tradition of some of the most esteemed restaurants and inns around the world. We now feature more complex dishes and more thoughtful presentations than I ever would have been able to offer in the high-pressure environment of the original restaurant. Our loyal customers have supported us through the change and have never stopped calling for reservations.

We still believe the dinner service is an integral part of the country inn experience we offer our guests. But we're now able to enjoy it again, which brings a renewed enthusiasm to what we do. Over the past few years, I've had several serious offers to give up the inn and open a "real" restaurant in Philadelphia. Although it's quite a compliment, I've never been tempted to say yes. Our dinner service strikes that delicate balance of interesting, well-prepared food, refined service, and an elegant setting—and I believe that's about as "real" as a restaurant gets.

Roasted Yellow Pepper Soup
with Garlic Cream

The intense flavor of roasted yellow peppers is balanced with a fresh garlic cream in this delicious hot soup. The contrasting swirl of the white garlic cream makes an elegant presentation. I prefer to use chicken stock for a richer flavor, but vegetable stock may be substituted for a strictly vegetarian version.

---

4 heads garlic, roasted (see Note)

1 cup Simple Crème Fraîche
     (page 17)

6 yellow bell peppers, roasted,
     peeled, and seeded (see Note)

3 cups Basic Chicken or Simple
     Vegetable Stock
     (pages 87, 91)

½ cup unsalted butter

¼ cup finely chopped onion

½ teaspoon white pepper

Salt to taste

---

1. Combine the garlic and the crème fraîche in a food processor or blender, and puree; set aside. Then puree the roasted peppers and chicken stock until smooth.

2. Melt the butter in a medium saucepan. Add the onions and sauté until translucent. Add the pepper puree and the white pepper and salt to taste, and bring just to a boil. Meanwhile, heat the garlic cream in a small saucepan until hot but not boiling. Divide the yellow pepper soup among six bowls, and swirl in the warm garlic cream, forming a decorative design. Serve immediately.

NOTE: To roast the garlic, preheat the oven to 350°F. Slice off the top ¼ inch of a large head of garlic, and drizzle a little extra virgin olive oil over it. Place the garlic in a glass baking pan and roast for 1 hour, until the cloves are soft.

To roast peppers, place the peppers over an open flame or under a broiler, turning them until all the skin has turned black. Seal the peppers in a brown paper bag and let them cool. Then peel off the charred skins.

This soup may be made up to 24 hours in advance, refrigerated, and reheated just before serving.

Simple Vegetable Stock

MAKES ABOUT 2 QUARTS

1 leek, thoroughly washed and
coarsely chopped
3 carrots, coarsely chopped
4 celery stalks, coarsely chopped
1 turnip, coarsely chopped

2 cloves garlic, peeled
4 flat-leaf parsley sprigs
4 thyme sprigs
2 bay leaves

Put all the ingredients in a large stockpot, add 4 quarts water, and bring to a boil. Then lower the heat to a simmer and cook for 1½ hours. Strain the stock through a fine-mesh sieve set over a bowl. The stock may be stored in the refrigerator for up to 2 days or in the freezer for up to 3 months.

Decorating the Inn

Guests often ask me, "Did you do all the decorating?" I am pleased to answer with an emphatic "Yes!" One of the most frequent compliments we receive from guests is how much they've enjoyed the inn's decor. I have a great time decorating the inn—it's fun. I get to choose the color schemes, pick out accent pieces, even select the coffee table books. I get to go shopping as part of my job!

One of the most personal elements is the array of Bob's photographs of the area that graces the inn's walls. Smaller ones complement the guest rooms' decor, while larger photos are the main visual element in the dining rooms. Some of our diners have assumed that we invite different photographers to feature their work here, but Bob is quick to let them know that he is the art committee. Although Bob may hold a monopoly on the gallery space, as art director I get to select which photographs are displayed. Knowing the artist personally means I get quite a good deal too, which was particularly important early on, when our budget was stretched.

It has taken us years to acquire the smaller decorative items that make the rooms look finished and make each one unique. I've purchased some pieces knowing exactly where I'd place them. Others were taken from room to room until I found a gap in the decor that needed filling. For a long time, I seemed to be always looking for items for the inn, scanning small boutiques, antiques stores, and mail-order catalogs. There was always a niche that needed to be filled and a place to put one more thing.

Lately, though, the inn's decor seems to be complete. Handcrafted folk art, antique accents, and traditional decor make the guest rooms pleasant to look at and comfortable to hang out in. The muted contemporary decor of the suites creates an oasis of calm—so much so that some of our suite guests never even go out.

Having been open for more than a decade, we're now giving less attention to adding new elements and more to maintaining or replacing existing ones, like installing new carpet. I'm still interested in acquiring new art pieces or antiques, but I'm much more selective now. The decor flows seamlessly from one area to the next. Sometimes it's something as small as a carefully placed pillow or an accent rug that pulls all the design elements together. But it all really works to create a beautiful finished effect.

Of course it's very satisfying to have the inn looking so lovely and to have our guests enjoy it so much. The only downside is that I don't get to do much shopping any more. There's only one thing to do, I suppose—I'll just have to redecorate!

Roasted Butternut Squash Soup

SERVES 6

Roasted winter squash gives a complex flavor to an easily prepared soup.

---

2 butternut squash
4 cups Basic Chicken or Simple
    Vegetable Stock (pages 87, 91)
½ cup unsalted butter
½ cup chopped onion

2 tablespoons minced fresh ginger
1 teaspoon ground cinnamon
½ teaspoon salt
Freshly grated nutmeg

---

1. Preheat the oven to 350°F.

2. Cut the squash in half and scoop out the seeds. Place the squash in a roasting pan, cover with foil, and roast for 1 hour, until tender. Then scoop out the pulp and discard the rinds. Combine the squash with 1 cup of the chicken stock in a food processor or blender, and process until smooth.

3. Melt the butter in a medium saucepan. Add the onions and fresh ginger, and cook over low heat for 2 minutes. Whisk in the squash puree, remaining 3 cups stock, the cinnamon, and salt, and bring to a boil. Grate some nutmeg over the soup before serving.

NOTE: The soup may be made up to 24 hours in advance, refrigerated, and reheated just before serving.

Dressed-Up Soups

• Float a swirl of chive or truffle oil on top of the soup.

• Use tiny cookie cutters to make shapes from extra pieces of puff pastry. Bake them and use as croutons.

• Whisk together crème fraîche and chopped herbs, and swirl a dollop into any savory cream soup.

• Add a scoop of granita or sorbet to turn a fruit soup into a refreshing dessert.

• Line individual bowls with slices of toasted French or Italian bread to form a base for gazpacho.

• Serve winter squash or pumpkin soups in hollowed-out mini-pumpkins, or use one large pumpkin for a buffet.

Scallop and Sweet Corn Chowder

When sweet corn is at its peak season, I buy extra ears to use later on in this hearty winter soup. So-called dry scallops are not treated with water-retaining preservatives, so they are a fresher product that will not release excess water when cooked. They are slightly more expensive, but do not include the up to 25 percent extra water weight that treated scallops absorb.

¼ cup unsalted butter

1 small onion, coarsely chopped

3 carrots, finely chopped

2 celery stalks, finely chopped

¼ cup all-purpose flour

½ cup dry white wine

1 cup Simple Fish Stock (page 88) or clam juice

2 thyme sprigs

½ teaspoon black pepper

¼ teaspoon cayenne pepper

3 small potatoes, peeled and cut into ¼-inch dice

24 large dry sea scallops

1 cup sweet corn kernels, fresh or frozen

2½ cups half-and-half

¼ cup dry sherry

2 tablespoons chopped flat-leaf parsley

Melt the butter in a large saucepan. Add the onions, carrots, and celery and cook over low heat until the vegetables are soft, 8 to 10 minutes. Whisk in the flour and cook for 2 minutes. Add the wine, stock, thyme, black and cayenne peppers, and 2 cups water. Add the potatoes and bring the mixture to a boil. Simmer until the potatoes are tender, stirring often to prevent sticking, about 8 minutes. Add the scallops and corn and cook for 2 minutes. Stir in the half-and-half and bring just to a boil. Remove from the heat and stir in the sherry and parsley. Divide the soup among six warm bowls, distributing the scallops evenly.

NOTE: This soup is best made just before serving because the scallops may toughen if reheated.

Oyster and Pancetta Chowder

Oysters and pancetta intermingle flavors in this slightly smoky chowder. Be careful to add the oysters just before serving to avoid their becoming tough.

---

6 slices pancetta, coarsely
  chopped
1 quart shucked oysters with their
  juices
½ cup unsalted butter
2 shallots, finely chopped
2 carrots, finely chopped

3 small potatoes, peeled and cut
  into ¼-inch dice
2 cups heavy cream
2 cups milk
½ teaspoon ground nutmeg
Salt and pepper to taste
¼ cup chopped flat-leaf parsley

---

1. Sauté the pancetta in a large skillet until crisp, turning once, 8 to 10 minutes, then drain on paper towels.

2. Drain the oysters, reserving the juices.

3. Melt the butter in a large saucepan. Add the shallots and carrots and cook over low heat until the vegetables are soft, 8 to 10 minutes. Add the oyster juices, potatoes, pancetta, and enough water to just cover the potatoes. Bring the mixture to a boil, then reduce the heat. Simmer until the potatoes are tender, stirring often to prevent sticking, about 8 minutes.

4. Add the cream, milk, and nutmeg and bring just to a boil. Add the oysters and cook for 1 minute. Remove from the heat and season to taste. Divide the soup among six warmed bowls, sprinkle with the parsley, and serve.

Apple Cheddar Soup

The unlikely soup combination of apples and cheddar will surprise even the greatest skeptic. Use a good-quality Vermont cheddar, such as the one from Shelburne Farms, for the rich savory bite that it adds to the soup.

---

6 apples, peeled, cored, and sliced, such as McIntosh
1 teaspoon ground cinnamon
2 cups half-and-half
½ cup unsalted butter
¼ cup chopped onion

3 tablespoons all-purpose flour
4 cups Basic Chicken Stock (page 87)
1 teaspoon salt
1 cup shredded cheddar

---

1. Combine the apples, cinnamon, and 1 cup of the half-and-half in a food processor or blender, and process until smooth.

2. Melt the butter in a medium saucepan. Add the onions and sauté on low heat until translucent, 3 minutes. Whisk in the flour and cook for 2 minutes. Whisk in the stock, salt, apple puree, and remaining 1 cup half-and-half. Bring just to a boil and remove from the heat. Stir in the cheddar until completely melted and incorporated. Serve warm.

NOTE: The soup may be made up to 24 hours in advance, stored in the refrigerator, and reheated just before serving.

Autumn at the Inn Means . . .

Gearing up emotionally to face a nonstop flow of guests.

Saying a sad good-bye to tomatoes from the garden.

Turning off the air-conditioning and enjoying fresh air again.

Preparing more roasted meats and baking more often.

Phasing out summer flavors like those of basil, sweet corn, and zucchini.

Picking the last of the berries and watching the canes turn brown and bare.

Watching the foliage gradually change color in our view behind the inn.

Mowing and weeding less frequently, and pulling out all the summer annuals.

Storing the wrought-iron and wicker furniture in the barn.

Including apples, cranberries, and winter squash on the menus.

Answering repeated phone queries: "When's the best time to see the foliage?"

Ordering firewood and having the chimneys cleaned and the stoves checked.

Picking up pumpkins at the farm stands and cutting corn stalks from our neighbor's field.

Seeing our trees drop their leaves in waves—first the birches, then the oaks and lindens, next the maples and balding cypress, and finally the weeping beech.

Hiring the local Amish boys to rake up all the leaves and wondering how they'll ever do it.

Pumpkin Soup with
Cinnamon Crème Fraîche

SERVES 6

In most pumpkin soup recipes the pumpkin is first roasted, but in this version, it is softened on the stovetop for a quicker solution. The combination of pumpkin with sautéed mushrooms and cinnamon cream is exquisite.

---

3 tablespoons extra virgin olive oil
1 pound fresh pumpkin, peeled, seeded, and cubed (see page 211)
1 small onion, finely chopped
2 cups Basic Chicken Stock (page 87)
8 tablespoons unsalted butter
½ pound chanterelle or other mushrooms, chopped

1 shallot, peeled and minced
2 tablespoons chopped flat-leaf parsley
½ cup heavy cream, whipped to soft peaks
Salt and pepper to taste
1 cup Simple Crème Fraîche (page 17)
1 teaspoon ground cinnamon

---

1. Heat the olive oil in a large skillet. Add the pumpkin and onions, and sauté on low heat until the pumpkin is softened, about 5 minutes. Pour in 1 cup of the stock and continue cooking until the pumpkin is very soft, about 10 minutes. Let cool slightly, then puree in a food processor and reserve.

2. Melt 1 tablespoon of the butter in a medium skillet. Add the mushrooms and shallots and cook over high heat until they are soft and all the liquid has evaporated, 4 to 5 minutes. Remove from the heat and stir in 2 tablespoons of the butter and the parsley. Keep warm.

3. Combine the pumpkin puree and the remaining 1 cup chicken stock in a large saucepan and bring to a simmer. Stir in the remaining 5 tablespoons butter, the whipped cream, and the reserved mushroom mixture. Adjust the seasoning to taste.

4. In a bowl, whisk together the crème fraîche and the cinnamon. Swirl this into the hot soup, and serve.

Chicken Corn Soup

I like the hearty Pennsylvania Dutch combination of chicken and corn in a saffron-scented broth, but my version leaves out the doughy "rivels"—a sort of rolled dumpling—that the traditional recipe calls for. Simmering the corncobs with the chicken creates a flavorful, slightly sweet base.

---

12 ears corn

2 whole bone-in chicken breasts
(with skin)

1 small onion, quartered

2 carrots, coarsely chopped

2 celery stalks, coarsely chopped

2 thyme sprigs

1 bay leaf

2 flat-leaf parsley sprigs

Pinch of saffron

3 cups Basic Chicken Stock
(page 87)

3 cups water

Salt to taste

3 hard-boiled eggs, coarsely
chopped

---

1. Bring enough water to a boil in a large pot to just cover 6 ears of corn. Add 6 ears of corn and cook for 7 minutes. Immediately drain the corn and submerge it in ice water to cool rapidly; then set aside. Break the remaining 6 ears of corn in half.

2. Place the chicken, onion, carrots, celery, thyme, bay leaf, parsley, saffron, stock, uncooked ears of corn (12 pieces), and water in a stockpot and bring to a boil. Reduce the heat to a simmer and cook for 45 minutes, until the chicken is cooked through, skimming the surface of the soup every 10 minutes or so to remove any fat or impurities. Strain the soup through a large colander into another large soup pot, and allow the strained liquid to settle for 5 minutes.

3. In the meantime, remove the chicken from the colander and discard the vegetables. Remove the meat from the chicken bones and discard the bones and skin. Cut the chicken meat into bite-size pieces. Drain the cooked whole ears of corn, and cut the kernels off the cobs.

4. Skim any remaining fat from the soup, and add the chicken pieces and corn kernels. Reheat the soup, and season to taste. Divide it evenly among six warmed bowls, and garnish with the chopped egg.

NOTE: The soup may be made up to 24 hours in advance, refrigerated, and reheated just before serving. Add cooked egg noodles for a heartier version.

Smoked Tomato Soup

SERVES 6

In the summertime, we have so many wonderful fresh tomatoes that I am always looking for new ways to prepare them. Using a stovetop smoker is a great way to add smoky complexity to basic tomato soup. The smoker looks like a metal steam-table tray with a tight-fitting lid and a raised rack inside. Small wood chips of alder or mesquite are scattered on the bottom, and the items you want to smoke (fish, vegetables, etc.) are placed on the rack. The tightly sealed metal tray is set on the stovetop over medium heat. The wood chips smolder to create enough smoke to add flavor. I was a little skeptical when I first purchased the smoker, but I have been delighted with the way it works. If you don't have a stovetop smoker, you can get the same results by using a standard smoker or by adding smoking chips to a covered outdoor grill.

---

18 red or yellow plum tomatoes, cored

½ cup unsalted butter

1 small onion, coarsely chopped

6 cups Basic Chicken or Simple Vegetable Stock (pages 87, 91)

Salt to taste

Coarsely ground pepper

---

1. Cut the tomatoes in half, and remove and discard the seeds. Place the tomatoes in a stovetop smoker and smoke until soft, 20 to 30 minutes. (If you don't have a smoker, use an outdoor grill. Soak the smoking chips for at least an hour. Add to the charcoal and replace the grill rack. Place the prepared tomatoes on a rack set over a baking sheet, set the sheet on the rack, and replace the lid, keeping the circulation holes closed. Smoke until the tomatoes are soft, 20 to 30 minutes.) Drain off any watery liquid, and crush the tomatoes in a food mill set over a bowl until only skins remain. Discard the skins.

2. Heat the butter in a large saucepan. Add the onions and sauté until translucent. Add the stock and the smoked tomato puree, and cook until just heated through. Season with salt to taste. Serve the soup in warmed bowls, garnished with coarsely ground pepper.

NOTE: The soup may be made up to 24 hours in advance, refrigerated, and reheated just before serving.

Tomato and Crab Soup with Basil

SERVES 6

Sweet, juicy plum tomatoes fresh from our garden require little embellishment to make a wonderful soup. I add fresh basil and crab here to complete the summer taste. The heavy cream makes a richer soup, but it's strictly optional.

---

18 red plum tomatoes, cored
1 teaspoon salt
6 basil leaves
½ cup unsalted butter
1 small onion, coarsely chopped
6 cups Basic Chicken or Simple
    Vegetable Stock (pages 87, 91)

½ teaspoon cayenne pepper
1 pound cooked lump or jumbo
    lump crabmeat
½ cup heavy cream (optional)
Salt and pepper to taste

---

1. Cut the tomatoes in half lengthwise, and remove and discard the seeds. Sprinkle the tomatoes with the salt. Place the tomatoes in a medium saucepan and add the basil. Cook for 10 minutes over medium heat, stirring often in the beginning to prevent sticking. Drain off any watery liquid, and crush the tomatoes in a food mill set over a bowl until only skins remain. Discard the skins.

2. Heat the butter in a large saucepan. Add the onions and sauté over low heat until translucent, 4 to 5 minutes. Add the stock, tomato puree, and cayenne pepper, and cook until just heated through, 5 to 7 minutes. Stir in the crabmeat and cook for 2 minutes. Add the cream if using, and season to taste. Serve hot.

NOTE: This soup may be made up to 24 hours in advance, refrigerated, and reheated just before serving.

SALADS

We've always offered an interesting array of salads that go beyond a simple mix of greens. Most of these salads are offered as a second or third course on our dinner menus, so they need to be intriguing yet compatible with the other dishes offered. Some of the more substantial salads were created to round out brunch menus or as main courses for catered luncheons. There's also a selection of salads that are excellent as a first course for dinner, especially during warmer weather.

We grow a wide variety of tender and piquant greens to incorporate into our salads. You may want to try growing your own fresh greens in your garden or in a window box, since most varieties germinate rapidly and are ready for harvest in about thirty days. Lettuces grow best in cool weather and require even watering. Select "cut and come again" varieties for a continuous harvest.

Spinach with Pancetta and Shallot-Gorgonzola Vinaigrette

The key to this flavorful dressing lies in caramelizing the shallots and serving the dressing slightly warmed. Instead of the scrambled eggs, a single poached quail egg nestled in the center of the greens would be an elegant touch.

---

6 thin slices pancetta

1 tablespoon unsalted butter

2 large eggs

1 cup extra virgin olive oil

2 shallots, finely chopped

½ cup white wine

3 tablespoons white wine vinegar

¼ cup crumbled Gorgonzola

2 tablespoons chopped flat-leaf parsley

2 pounds baby spinach

---

1. Sauté the pancetta in a large skillet over medium heat until crisp on both sides, 8 to 10 minutes. Drain on paper towels, then crumble and set aside.

2. Melt the butter in a medium skillet over low heat. Whisk the eggs together in a small bowl, pour into the skillet, and scramble until just cooked through. Set aside.

3. Heat ½ cup of the olive oil in a medium skillet. Add the shallots and sauté over low heat until golden (not brown), 6 to 8 minutes. Add the wine and cook until reduced by half, about 2 minutes. Remove the skillet from the heat and stir in the remaining ½ cup olive oil. Allow to cool slightly.

4. Combine the shallot mixture, vinegar, Gorgonzola, and parsley in a food processor and pulse briefly until just combined. Toss the spinach with the warm shallot dressing. Divide the spinach among six individual plates. Spoon the scrambled eggs into the center of the spinach and top with the crumbled pancetta. Serve immediately.

NOTE: The dressing may be made up to 48 hours in advance, refrigerated, and reheated just before serving. Salad may be served on one large platter.

Growing Spinach for Salads

We grow tender baby spinach for our salads in raised beds. Spinach grows best in cool weather, so we start some in early spring and then plant again in late summer. It tolerates sudden dips in temperature, especially when protected with a blanket or an agri-cover (available in gardening catalogs). All spinach is not created equal, however. The typical baby spinach found in markets is not just a smaller version of regular spinach but a special variety without a lot of veining and crinkling. Smooth-leafed spinach is easier to wash, making it perfect for salads. I like a Dutch variety called Wolter. It produces smooth almond-shaped leaves and has a mild flavor that's delicious in salads.

Poached Pears with Stilton and Belgian Endive

SERVES 6

This salad always gets raves when we serve it at dinner, for both appearance and taste. The pears are poached ahead of time, then filled with a blend of Stilton and cream cheese and warmed in the oven until the cheese softens. The lettuces are tossed with a savory pear vinaigrette, and a warm stuffed pear is placed in the center of each serving. If you like, add a sprinkling of toasted walnuts.

½ cup sugar	2 tablespoons extra virgin olive oil
1 tablespoon fresh lemon juice	½ cup corn or vegetable oil
4 Bosc or Comice pears, peeled	1 head Boston lettuce, leaves
½ cup crumbled Stilton	separated
4 ounces cream cheese, softened	2 heads Belgian endive, leaves
3 tablespoons white wine vinegar	separated
½ teaspoon chopped thyme	½ cup walnuts, toasted (optional)

---

1. Combine the sugar, lemon juice, and 4 cups water in a medium saucepan, and bring the mixture to a boil. Add the pears and simmer for 12 to 15 minutes, until fork-tender. Allow the pears to cool in the liquid.

2. Preheat the oven to 350°F.

3. When you're ready to serve, combine the Stilton and the cream cheese in a food processor, and process until smooth. Cut three of the pears in half. Remove the seeds and core, creating a small cavity in each pear half for the cheese filling. Place the pears, cut side up, on a baking sheet and divide the filling among the six halves. Bake for 8 to 10 minutes, until the filling is heated through and just beginning to brown. Remove the pears from the oven and allow them to cool slightly.

4. While the pears are baking, core the remaining pear and chop it into small pieces. Combine the pear pieces, vinegar, and thyme in a food processor, and puree. Slowly add the olive oil and corn oil, processing until thickened.

5. In a mixing bowl, toss the Boston lettuce with the pear vinaigrette. Arrange the endive leaves in a fan pattern on six plates, and mound the lettuce in the center. Place a baked pear in the center of each plate, and garnish with toasted walnuts if desired.

NOTE: The vinaigrette may be prepared up to 48 hours in advance. The poached pears may be held in their poaching liquid in the refrigerator for up to 48 hours.

Washing Lettuce

All of these salad recipes assume that you will wash the ingredients first (yes, even those bagged lettuces that are prewashed). Submerging lettuce in cold water refreshes it, even if it is already clean. To wash lettuce, fill a large bowl with cold water. Place just as much lettuce in the bowl as will allow you to swirl it around effectively. Remove the lettuce by hand and set it in a colander to drain. Repeat the process as necessary until the lettuce is completely clean, then spin it dry in a salad spinner (or if you don't own a salad spinner, put the lettuce in a large cotton pillowcase and toss it dry). Roll the lettuce up in paper towels and then seal it in airtight plastic bags until ready to use, up to 48 hours in advance for leafy lettuces. Tender baby greens require a light touch in the spinner, because they bruise easily. Don't wash baby greens until just before you're ready to use them, because refrigerating them with any remaining trace of water will make them spoil more quickly.

NOTES FROM THE INN:
THE GUEST COMMENT SHEET

We find it useful to ask our guests for their comments about their stay. Unlike the typical hotel comment survey eliciting just complaints, I've designed a questionnaire that gives guests the opportunity to tell us what they enjoyed as well. I refer to this as the "I'm O.K., You're O.K." survey, which lets us know what we're doing right and what areas need our attention. It also makes it easier for our best customers, guests who've enjoyed their stay and might not want to offend us with negative comments, to let us know if there are any areas that need improvement.

The first line reads "One thing I really enjoyed about my stay is . . ." and the guests fill in the blank. Typically the responses include the food, the decor, the cleanliness, and the innkeepers (Bob thinks this means him). The second line, which reads "One thing that would have made my stay more enjoyable is . . .," often elicits a positive response too, like "staying longer," or something beyond our control, like "better weather."

We've received many helpful ideas from guests about things that seem obvious once they've been pointed out to us, such as adding full-length mirrors to the guest rooms, supplying reading lamps for every chair, offering a low-calorie breakfast choice, and putting radio/alarm clocks in all of the rooms. Sometimes the ideas they suggest might seem ideal for the guests but don't work for us—later check-out time, serving breakfast until noon, or having a variety of newspapers available.

But sometimes the comments are just plain weird. On a sweltering 100-degree weekend in July, one person complained that they were disappointed they could not use the gas fireplace (this same person also noted that the air conditioning wasn't cold enough). One guest wrote a two-page dissertation on why we should include free coffee with dinner. We've been told that our mattresses are too firm or not firm enough, our pillows are too fluffy or too flat. One guest complained that our windows were not sufficiently insulated to block out the "clatter" of the horses and buggies going by on Sunday morning.

In spite of the sometimes unusual responses, the great majority of our guests' comments are very helpful. I find it amazing that some innkeepers will subject themselves to agency ratings but never think to ask their own customers for a critique. Guests who leave comments have actually stayed at our inn and essentially have made an investment in our business. By soliciting their comments, we're getting free advice on how to improve our business, by either refining our services or ensuring that our marketing efforts are accurate. Bringing in a professional to review our facility would certainly cost more, and we'd probably never get to appreciate how much most of our guests really do enjoy their stay. As for the "clatter" of the horses and buggies, I think it's one of those things our guests may just have to get used to.

A Trio of Summer Salads
with Balsamic Vinegar

SERVES 6

This is my standard summer salad when the tomatoes and green beans are at their prolific peak in the garden. Use a variety of shapes and colors of cherry tomatoes if you can. In keeping with the informality of summer, the three salads are served on a single platter. For individual service, I arrange the various elements on thick slabs of glass and add a toasted crouton topped with crumbled goat cheese for a dramatic presentation.

½ cup extra virgin olive oil	½ pound fresh haricots verts,
3 tablespoons balsamic vinegar	stem ends trimmed
2 garlic cloves	1 small shallot, finely chopped
¾ cup basil leaves	2 pints cherry tomatoes
6 Japanese eggplants	2 tablespoons chopped onion
Salt	¼ cup calamata olives, chopped

1. Combine the olive oil, vinegar, garlic, and ½ cup of the basil in a food processor or blender, and process until combined.

2. Preheat a grill or broiler.

3. Trim off the ends of the eggplants, and slice the eggplants lengthwise into ⅛-inch-thick strips. Brush the eggplant strips with some of the vinaigrette, and grill them briefly until softened but not browned, about 1½ minutes per side (watch them carefully—they can brown quickly and turn bitter). Allow the eggplant to cool, then refrigerate until thoroughly chilled.

4. Fill a medium skillet with water, lightly salt it, and bring to a boil. Add the haricots verts and cook just until brightly colored, 1 to 1½ minutes. Immediately drain the beans and plunge them into ice water until thoroughly cooled. Drain the beans, toss them with the shallots in a bowl, and refrigerate until thoroughly chilled.

5. Cut the cherry tomatoes in half and toss with the onions. Slice the remaining ¼ cup basil into thin ribbons.

6. Toss the eggplant strips with the olives, and arrange on one third of a large platter. Arrange the haricots verts and tomatoes separately on the platter. Drizzle the remaining vinaigrette over all, sprinkle the basil ribbons over the salads, and serve.

NOTE: The eggplants and haricots verts may be prepared up to 8 hours ahead of time and refrigerated until ready to serve.

Growing Cherry Tomatoes

Even if you have only a tiny balcony or a small yard, you can grow cherry tomatoes in containers and enjoy them all summer long. The most interesting varieties are unavailable as plants and must be grown indoors from seed, starting about eight weeks before the last frost date in your area. They sprout quickly and grow rapidly into tall plants. Some of our recent favorite varieties include Yellow Pear, a golden teardrop-shaped tomato; Camp Joy, large round red cherries; and Sungold, a prolific golden orange variety with a round shape. Once they're off to a good start, support the plants with stakes and give them plenty of sunlight, and you'll have a bounteous crop. Container plants require consistent watering because they have so little soil mass to draw moisture from. If you plant cherry tomatoes in your garden, watch where any of the fruit falls because the seeds will easily germinate the following year, perhaps in places you don't want them. We recently had a bonus crop of Camp Joy near our mulch pile, where the plants that were added to the compost the year before had reseeded and grew unaided along the fence.

From the Garden

While we enjoy growing our own specialty produce in season, we can't rely on our garden alone for a sufficient supply of fruits and vegetables. Our country location is a great benefit because of the availability of fresh produce in season. Most of the local farmers sell homegrown produce at their own farm stands, so an array of freshly picked fruits and vegetables is available from late April until early November. In addition to the fresh produce, the local Mennonite and Amish women are renowned for their canning and preserving abilities. Gingham-topped jars of bread-and-butter pickles, strawberry-rhubarb jam, and corn relish are among my favorite finds. Every morning before the sun heats ups, I visit the stands for the best selection. The fresh juicy peaches from the orchard down the road are legendary with our guests. Sweet corn, cantaloupes, and zucchini are abundant and delicious. Fall crops such as pumpkins and apples mark the end of the season. Once the last farm stand has closed, it becomes more difficult to secure the produce we need. But even in the country, we can get overnight delivery of these items. I've found a specialty produce broker who will arrange to ship what we need directly from the growers, ensuring that we receive fresh produce the morning after it's harvested.

Minted Strawberry Salad
with Balsamic Vinegar

Strawberry and mint are a natural pairing that is enlivened with good-quality balsamic vinegar. For the best results, you'll need to invest in a bottle of aged balsamic vinegar at a specialty store and avoid the (usually rancid) versions sold at supermarkets. Although it may seem expensive, a little bit goes a long way in adding flavor. We sometimes serve this salad on individual Belgian endive leaves paired with fresh creamy Brie as a cheese course following an early summer dinner.

---

1 quart chilled strawberries, hulled and quartered

¼ cup walnuts, toasted and coarsely chopped

¼ cup finely chopped sweet onion

3 tablespoons chopped mint

4 tablespoons balsamic vinegar

3 tablespoons extra virgin olive oil

3 heads Belgian endive, leaves separated

---

1. In a bowl, toss together the strawberries, walnuts, onions, and mint. Sprinkle 3 tablespoons of the balsamic vinegar over the mixture, and toss briefly until just combined.

2. In another bowl, combine the olive oil and remaining 1 tablespoon vinegar, and toss with the endive leaves. Arrange five or six endive leaves in a circle, tips outward, on each of six chilled plates. Spoon the strawberry mixture into the center, and serve.

NOTE: This salad is best prepared just before serving.

Marinated Green Beans with Crispy Leeks

SERVES 6

We grow haricots verts in our garden and try our best to pick them at their intended tiny size. Often we miss some until they've grown a little too much. The fresh flavor of the beans is still there, and a little marinade tenderizes the larger beans and makes this wonderful summertime salad. A crisp topping of briefly fried leeks creates an interesting combination of textures and flavors.

---

1 pound tender green beans, stem
    ends removed
1 shallot, finely chopped
¼ cup extra virgin olive oil
1 tablespoon white wine vinegar
2 tablespoons fresh lemon juice
1 teaspoon grated lemon zest

1 teaspoon grated fresh horseradish
2 tablespoons chopped tarragon
2 leeks, white parts only,
    thoroughly washed
¼ cup vegetable oil
Salt to taste
Calendula flower petals (optional)

---

1. Bring lightly salted water to a boil in a medium skillet. Add the green beans and cook just until brightly colored and tender, 1½ to 3 minutes. Immediately drain the beans and plunge them into ice water until thoroughly cooled.

2. Combine the shallots, olive oil, vinegar, lemon juice, lemon zest, horseradish, and tarragon in a food processor or blender, and process until smooth. Toss the beans with the vinaigrette in a bowl, and refrigerate until serving.

3. Cut the leeks into julienne and roll in paper towels to dry completely. Heat the vegetable oil in a medium skillet. Add the leeks and fry until golden, about 3 minutes. Remove with a slotted spoon, drain on paper towels, and season with salt to taste.

4. Divide the beans among six plates, top with the crispy leeks, and add the calendula petals if desired. Serve immediately.

NOTE: The beans may be tossed with the vinaigrette and refrigerated up to 2 hours before serving—but no longer or they will lose their crispness. The leeks may be fried ahead of time and then recrisped on a cookie sheet in a 325°F oven for 2 to 3 minutes.

Asparagus and Watercress
with Chive Vinaigrette

This salad combines two of my favorite spring vegetables with my favorite spring herb. Purple chive flowers have an intense chive flavor and may be sprinkled sparingly on top for a beautiful look. When choosing asparagus, don't assume that a thinner stalk means the asparagus is younger. Often the super-thin stalks are merely the end of the harvest and may in fact not be as tender as fatter ones picked earlier in the season. Chervil is a fernlike spring green that adds a fragrant anise scent.

---

30 asparagus spears (about 1½ pounds)	1 teaspoon grated lemon zest
2 tablespoons minced chives plus 6 long whole chives	½ teaspoon coarsely ground pepper
¼ cup extra virgin olive oil	2 bunches watercress, stems removed
3 tablespoons fresh lemon juice	¼ cup crumbled goat cheese, about 4 ounces (optional)
2 tablespoons chopped chervil or flat-leaf parsley	

---

1. Trim the woody ends off the asparagus and discard. Peel the asparagus spears, cut them in half lengthwise, and set them aside.

2. Bring lightly salted water to a boil in a medium skillet. Add the whole chives and simmer until they turn bright green and just limp, about 20 seconds. Immediately remove the chives from the water and submerge them in ice water. Add the asparagus halves to the simmering water and cook until they are bright green and tender, about 2 minutes. Immediately remove the asparagus and submerge them in ice water to chill thoroughly. Drain well.

3. Combine the olive oil, lemon juice, chervil, minced chives, lemon zest, and pepper in a small bowl and whisk to blend. Place the cooled asparagus in a dish and toss with half of the vinaigrette. Place the watercress in a bowl, and toss with the remaining vinaigrette. Tie ten asparagus halves in a bundle (with the tips pointing in one direction), using a blanched chive to tie them together around the center. Repeat with the remaining asparagus and chives. Divide the watercress among six chilled plates, and arrange the asparagus bundles on top. Top the asparagus with the crumbled cheese if desired, and serve.

VARIATION: For a more substantial entree salad, add shrimp sautéed in garlic and olive oil.

NOTE: The asparagus may be blanched up to 2 hours in advance and refrigerated. The vinaigrette may be made up to 8 hours in advance and refrigerated.

Asparagus and Belgian Endive
with Roquefort and Walnuts

SERVES 6

I had always found walnut oil bitter until I tasted it freshly pressed in the Périgord region of France, where it is a specialty. Walnut oil must be properly stored to retain its rich, nutty flavor and undoubtedly the oil I'd tasted before had turned rancid. As we dined by candlelight overlooking the Dordogne River, we were treated to a simple asparagus salad dressed with fragrant walnut oil. My version includes crisp endive and a little crumbled Roquefort as well.

---

30 medium asparagus spears (about 1 pound), trimmed
¼ cup extra virgin olive oil
2 tablespoons white wine vinegar
1 teaspoon minced shallots
½ cup crumbled Roquefort

2 tablespoons chopped dill
3 heads Belgian endive, leaves separated
2 tablespoons walnut oil
¼ cup walnut pieces, toasted

---

1. Bring lightly salted water to a boil in a medium-size skillet. Add the asparagus and simmer until bright green and tender, about 2 minutes. Immediately drain the asparagus and submerge them in ice water to chill thoroughly.

2. Combine the olive oil, vinegar, shallots, ¼ cup of the Roquefort, and the dill in a food processor, and process until smooth. Cut the Belgian endive leaves into lengthwise julienne, and toss with the vinaigrette.

3. Divide the endive among six chilled plates. Drain the asparagus tips, dry with paper towels, and toss with the walnut oil. Arrange the tips on top of the endive. Sprinkle the remaining ¼ cup Roquefort and the walnuts over the salad, and serve.

Spinach and Cantaloupe with Aged Goat Cheese and Pine Nuts

Sweet ripe cantaloupe is a perfect match for tangy aged goat cheese and fresh spinach. The pine nuts add texture to this refreshing summer salad. When aged, goat cheese acquires a firm texture, perfect for slicing.

½ cup extra virgin olive oil	2 pounds baby spinach
1 shallot, peeled and chopped	½ small cantaloupe, seeded
½ cup flat-leaf parsley leaves	8 ounces aged goat cheese
3 tablespoons white wine vinegar	¼ cup pine nuts, toasted

1. Combine the olive oil, shallot, parsley, and vinegar in a food processor, and process until smooth. In a mixing bowl, toss the spinach with about two thirds of the vinaigrette. Divide the spinach among six chilled plates.

2. Cut the cantaloupe into 1½-inch-thick slices, remove the rind, and then cut into ½- to ¾-inch cubes. Cut the goat cheese into approximately the same size pieces, and toss in a bowl with the cantaloupe and the remaining vinaigrette. Divide the cantaloupe and cheese among the plates, placing them in the center of the spinach. Sprinkle with the pine nuts, and serve.

NOTE: The vinaigrette may be made up to 24 hours in advance and refrigerated until ready to serve.

Cooking for a Crowd

Guests often ask how I learned to cook for so many people at one time. It reminds me of the riddle "How do you get to Carnegie Hall?" because the answer is the same: "Practice! Practice! Practice!" My greatest learning experience as a professional chef has been in the day-to-day operation of the inn.

My mom was my first and only culinary teacher. She taught me all the basics: how to draw up a food budget, how to choose quality ingredients, and how to time everything so all the parts of the meal are ready at the same time. She would have all the ingredients ready, explaining every step to me as she worked. Then she would hand me a spoon and let me help out, perhaps stirring the batter for a cake or tasting the soup to determine how much salt to add.

Cooking for a crowd of guests at our inn is a little more involved than making a family dinner, but it has the same starting point: organization. I've learned to have all my ingredients ready and to do as much advance preparation as possible. If you're not organized when orders start rolling in, you'll never catch up. Being in the weeds, as it's known, is a terrible feeling, so I've learned to avoid getting behind by being meticulous about having everything prepped when it's time to cook.

Spending most days in the kitchen has added to my expertise, improving my skills and building my confidence. Being driven to succeed has given me the added tenacity necessary to achieve excellence. I've realized that like so many facets of running an inn, cooking for a crowd is something that can't be learned in a classroom. In the words of the philosopher Syrus, "Practice is the best of all instructors."

Smoked Trout, Potatoes, and Pecans with Creamy Dill Dressing

SERVES 6

The combination of flavors and textures in this salad is sublime, bound together by a fresh dill dressing. Substitute small new potatoes if fingerlings are unavailable. The potatoes must be prepared ahead of time so they can chill thoroughly before the salad is assembled.

6 large fingerling potatoes, ends trimmed
1 large egg
1 cup corn oil
3 tablespoons white wine vinegar
¼ cup sour cream

¼ cup chopped dill
4 ounces smoked trout (about 1 fillet), skin removed
2 heads Boston lettuce, leaves separated
½ cup pecans, toasted

1. Slice the potatoes crosswise into ⅛-inch-thick pieces. Bring lightly salted water to a boil in a medium skillet. Add the potatoes and simmer until tender but not falling apart, 3 to 4 minutes. Immediately drain and allow to cool. Refrigerate until thoroughly chilled.

2. Process the egg in a food processor until light in color. Gradually drizzle in the corn oil, processing until it is well emulsified. Add the vinegar, sour cream, and dill, and process just to combine.

3. Crumble the trout into a small bowl. Add the potatoes, toss with about half of the dressing, and set aside. In another bowl, toss the lettuce with the remaining dressing. Arrange half of the lettuce in the center of individual chilled plates, and top with half of the trout mixture. Repeat to form two more layers. Sprinkle with the pecans, and serve.

Chicken and Apple Salad
with Creamy Cider Dressing

Several times a year I take a day off to meet my friend Maureen for lunch. No matter how upscale the restaurant we choose may be, we have a running joke that the menu can't be very good if it doesn't feature chicken salad. This tasty version uses autumn harvest apples, and toasted walnuts add a crisp bite. The chicken breasts are poached in the oven with cider and butter until tender.

3 whole boneless, skinless chicken breasts (about 1½ pounds)	3 tablespoons cider vinegar
3 cups apple cider	2 teaspoons chopped flat-leaf parsley
¼ cup unsalted butter, melted	¼ cup sour cream
½ teaspoon dried thyme	3 small apples, such as McIntosh
2 teaspoons ground cinnamon	½ cup walnuts, toasted
1 large egg	1 head Boston lettuce, leaves separated
½ cup corn oil	

1. Preheat the oven to 375°F.

2. Place the chicken breasts in a shallow glass pan, and pour 1 cup of the cider and the melted butter over them. Sprinkle with the thyme and 1 teaspoon of the cinnamon. Cover with foil and bake for 20 to 25 minutes, until cooked through. Allow to cool completely.

3. In the meantime, simmer the remaining 2 cups cider in a small saucepan until reduced by half, about 20 minutes. Allow to cool completely.

4. Process the egg in a food processor until light in color. Gradually drizzle in the corn oil, processing until it is well emulsified. Add the reduced cider, cider vinegar, parsley, sour cream, and remaining 1 teaspoon cinnamon, and process until combined.

5. Cut the chicken into bite-size pieces. Core the apples and slice them into thin pieces. In a large bowl, toss the chicken, apples, and walnuts with the dressing. Divide the lettuce among six chilled plates, top with the chicken salad, and serve.

NOTE: The chicken may be baked up to 24 hours in advance and refrigerated until ready to serve. The dressing may be made up to 24 hours in advance and refrigerated until ready to serve.

NOTES FROM THE INN:
THE COOKBOOK

Guests often wonder how I came to write my first cookbook. The story is an example of how you never know who your guests are. I don't ask probing questions of our guests, so I rarely know what line of work they're in unless they volunteer the information. A couple from New York who were "regulars"—they had stayed more than a couple of times at the inn—were enjoying breakfast one summer morning when they casually asked me if I had ever thought of doing a cookbook. I answered, "All the time!" Anyone who loves cookbooks as much as I do has thought about writing his or her own. The man told me that he was a literary agent. I knew nothing about the process of getting a book published, and I certainly didn't know what an agent did, but his question sounded like a compliment. The couple checked out and I thought that was the end of the matter. A few days later I received a few cookbooks authored by some of the chefs the agent represented. I was stunned—they were beautiful and all were written by well-known chefs.

When I called him, we talked about the type of book I wanted to write and I explained that I loved coffee table cookbooks with color photographs and personal musings of the chef. In his usual direct style, he said, "Well, forget it, because you're never going to get that kind of book published." The best I could hope for would be a small recipe book with perhaps some illustrations. We submitted a series of different proposals, and I gradually lined my office walls with rejection letters from the finest cookbook publishers in the country. Finally, an editor requested that I submit a proposal for a breakfast and brunch book with some of Bob's photographs of the area. The proposal was accepted. Once completed, it turned out to be the coffee table cookbook that I had dreamed of. I am still amazed every time I go into a bookstore and see it there.

Getting the book published was easy; the challenge was selling it. I had seen book signings by famous fiction writers, where people waited in line for hours to meet the author. It seemed pretty glamorous. The reality is that making appearances can be a grueling experience, especially with the added responsibility of bringing food samples, which is the best way for a little-known author to sell cookbooks. (I once did a signing at a well-known upscale cookware store that turned into a feeding frenzy. I was amazed that people would put something in their mouth without having any idea of what it was, just because it was free. I sold a lot of books that day, but it wasn't pretty.)

Even with the added obligations, being an author is still a great thrill for me. Because I'm so accessible at the inn, people often call me to talk about the book or to ask me a question about a recipe. We've had many guests come to the inn just because they had loved the book.

I also get a kick out of seeing my name on the bookstore poster announcing "Chef Donna Leahy will be signing her book here." I sometimes wonder how many people look at that poster and say, "Who?" But as long as even a few people line up to meet me just because they've enjoyed my work and my food, it's a good feeling. I'm always happy to chat with them while I sign their copy of the book. I've learned, however, to stay out of the way of the free samples.

Chicken and Pineapple Salad
with Almonds

SERVES 6

Fresh ripe pineapple is the key to this salad. Grilling the chicken adds a unique taste.

1 large egg	¼ cup extra virgin olive oil
½ cup corn oil	2 garlic cloves, minced
¼ cup pineapple juice	1 tablespoon Dijon mustard
2 tablespoons white wine vinegar	1 tablespoon fresh lemon juice
¼ cup low-fat yogurt	3 whole boneless, skinless chicken
¼ cup tarragon leaves	breasts (about 1½ pounds)
¼ cup chopped chives	3 small pineapples
¼ cup flat-leaf parsley leaves	½ cup slivered almonds, toasted
¼ teaspoon cayenne pepper	

1. Process the egg in a food processor until light in color. Gradually drizzle in the corn oil, processing until it is well emulsified. Add the pineapple juice, vinegar, yogurt, tarragon, chives, parsley, and cayenne pepper, and process until smooth. Set aside.

2. Preheat a grill or broiler.

3. Whisk the olive oil, garlic, mustard, and lemon juice together in a bowl. Toss the chicken breasts with the olive oil mixture, and grill the chicken until lightly browned and just cooked through, 5 to 7 minutes per side. Allow to cool, and then cut into bite-size pieces.

4. Slice the pineapples in half vertically, from the bottom all the way through the green top. Remove and discard the core. Hollow out the center to form a bowl for the chicken salad, reserving the fruit. Chop the reserved fruit into bite-size chunks. In a bowl, toss the pineapple chunks with the chicken and the reserved dressing. Divide the chicken salad among the six pineapple halves, sprinkle the almonds over the salad, and serve.

NOTE: The chicken salad may also be served over a bed of fresh greens, with toast points, or in hollowed-out toasted baguette halves, in lieu of the hollowed-out pineapples. The chicken may be cooked up to 24 hours in advance and refrigerated until ready to serve. The dressing may be prepared up to 24 hours in advance and refrigerated until ready to use.

Soft-Shell Crab Salad
with Citrus Vinaigrette

SERVES 6

Now that we serve a fixed menu for dinner, my menu planning involves trying to make sure that all of our diners are satisfied with the selections. Although I was a little reluctant to include soft-shell crabs at first, I decided to have our guests experience one of my favorite seasonal dishes in this salad flavored with fresh citrus. Many guests who have never tried soft-shells before are convinced with the first delicious bite.

1 cup extra virgin olive oil
1 shallot, peeled and minced
¼ cup flat-leaf parsley leaves
¼ cup fresh grapefruit juice
1 teaspoon fresh lemon juice
½ teaspoon sugar
2 tablespoons unsalted butter
6 soft-shell crabs, cleaned (ask the fishmonger to do this)

Flour for dredging
2 heads Boston lettuce, leaves separated
2 cups pea shoots or watercress leaves
2 grapefruit, peeled, seeded, and sectioned

1. Combine the olive oil, shallots, parsley, grapefruit juice, lemon juice, and sugar in a food processor or blender, and process until blended.

2. Melt the butter in a large skillet. Dip each of the soft-shells into the flour, lightly coating both sides, and add the crabs to the skillet. Sauté until golden brown and cooked through, 3 to 4 minutes per side.

3. Toss the lettuce and pea shoots with half of the vinaigrette, and divide the greens among six plates. Place a crab on each plate, and drizzle the remaining dressing over the crabs. Garnish with the grapefruit sections, and serve.

NOTE: The vinaigrette may be made up to 24 hours in advance and refrigerated until ready to use.

NOTES FROM THE INN:
THE RESERVATIONS BOOK

Even though I do a lot of my work on a computer, I just can't seem to trust it enough to put our reservations exclusively on a computer program. We hand-write all reservations in what we refer to simply as "The Book." It's easier for us than having a computer on all the time to check availability, and it allows us to double-check each other when reservations are made. Not that our system is perfect. One of the worst nightmares occurs when we accidentally overbook.

In the best cases, we catch the overbooking before the guests are scheduled to arrive, so we are able to call and inform them of our error. Sometimes the guests are really great about the whole thing, noting that "everyone makes mistakes." We offer them a full refund and a future complimentary stay with an upgrade where possible. Some guests are thrilled about it, as though they've won a prize. Others have gotten really angry. Once, on Christmas Eve, we realized that we had double-booked a suite for New Year's Eve. The woman who had originally booked the room told us she didn't want any freebies. "I bought the dress, and I'm coming!" she shouted. The other couple accepted a complimentary Valentine's Package for February and let us off the hook.

But in the worst cases (I think it happened twice, in the early years), the people arrive at the front desk to check in. You scan the list of expected guests, at first in disbelief. Then you realize that they have a confirmation in your handwriting—and you don't have them in The Book. It is a terrible moment. (I'm ashamed to say that at this point, we check to see whose handwriting it is so we know which one of us made the mistake! The innocent one is then free to be completely magnanimous.) Unlike a large hotel, we have no flexibility when we overbook. So we have to do everything we can to try to make it right for the guest, and this usually costs us a lot. Of course they get a full refund. If they wish, we arrange for them to stay in another inn in the area in a deluxe suite at our expense. We offer complimentary dinner at the inn as well. Plus, we give them a future complimentary stay at our inn.

When we go on vacation, we don't take The Book with us because we're afraid of losing it. The Book never leaves the inn. The simple question "I can't find The Book, have you seen it?" strikes fear into our hearts. But over the years, we've managed to be accurate almost all the time. So I think we'll stick with The Book. I did, however, just think of a compelling reason to put all of our reservations on the computer after all: When there is a mistake, we could be magnanimous and at the same time blame the error on a software glitch.

Quail with Belgian Endive and Blueberry Vinaigrette

SERVES 6

I like to use fresh quail in salads because they are just the right size. They also taste delicious, especially when grilled and paired with a fresh blueberry vinaigrette.

¼ cup plus 3 tablespoons extra virgin olive oil

1 teaspoon minced garlic

6 semi-boneless quail (ask the butcher to prepare them)

3 heads Belgian endive, leaves separated

2 tablespoons fresh lemon juice

½ cup blueberries

1. Preheat a grill or broiler.

2. Combine 2 tablespoons of the olive oil with the garlic, and brush this all over the quail. Grill the quail until lightly browned and cooked through, 3 to 4 minutes per side.

3. In the meantime, heat 1 tablespoon of the olive oil in a large skillet. Add the endive and cook until just wilted, 1 to 1½ minutes. Remove the endive to a warm plate and heat the remaining ¼ cup oil in the skillet. Stir in the lemon juice and blueberries and cook for 1 minute. Divide the endive among six warmed plates, and place a grilled quail on each. Spoon the warm blueberry vinaigrette over the quail, and serve.

Great Guests

As innkeepers, we've been fortunate to have met some terrific people. Some of our guests come only once, but others return year after year. When these returning guests arrive at our door, it's like welcoming back old friends or family members. Many hug us at the door and bring us gifts, as if they've arrived at a house party. Some of our cherished guests have become close personal friends.

Our guests come from all walks of life. Nearby Washington, D.C., has brought us a clientele of federal government executives, some with the National Security Agency. When I naively asked one of these guests what type of work it involved, he declared half-jokingly that if he told me, he'd have to kill me. One of our favorite customers flies in often from Silicon Valley to meet with software designers. He spends every evening he's here exactly the same way: unwinding on the back porch, smoking a cigar, and watching the sun set. We've had lawyers and doctors, cat fanciers and greyhound rescuers, chefs and innkeepers, teachers and retirees, stay-at-home moms and dads, famous and aspiring actors, network news crews and Hollywood film directors. No matter what line of work they're in, our favorite guests share our enthusiasm for great food and for the beauty of our area.

There's often a melancholy feeling when guests leave, as if they'd like to enjoy one more moment before returning to the "real world." One of our beloved guests honored us by requesting that some of his ashes be spread behind the inn upon his death, since he considered our inn his second home. We receive letters of thanks, photographs of babies and family members we've yet to meet, and holiday cards from around the world. Having an inn gives us the opportunity to meet new friends each time we welcome guests into our home.

Lobster Salad with Roasted Peaches

One of my favorite inns in France is L'Espérance, located in the beautiful rolling hills of Burgundy. We had four meals while staying there, each one more exquisite than the last. The chef's lobster salad was a triumph of summer flavors; my version humbly aspires to be the same.

---

4 large firm peaches, pitted, peeled, and sliced into wedges
4 tablespoons fresh lemon juice
1 tablespoon light brown sugar
2 tablespoons Madeira or dry sherry
2 tablespoons unsalted butter
3 live lobsters, 1½ pounds each

1 large egg
¾ cup corn oil
¼ cup flat-leaf parsley leaves
1 teaspoon chopped tarragon
½ teaspoon curry powder
1 pound mâche or arugula
½ pound frisée

---

1. Preheat the oven to 375°F.

2. Butter a glass 9 × 13-inch baking dish, and add the peaches. Sprinkle 2 tablespoons of the lemon juice, the brown sugar, and the Madeira over the peaches. Dot with the butter. Roast the peaches for 8 to 10 minutes, until beginning to turn golden but still firm. Let the peaches cool completely, then drain off the liquid.

3. Fill a lobster pot or large stockpot with 2 inches of water and bring to a boil. Plunge the lobsters into the boiling water, cover, and cook until they've just turned red, about 8 minutes. Remove the lobsters from the pot and immediately submerge them in ice water. Allow to cool.

4. Pull off the lobster claws and tails, and discard the bodies. Place the tails, hard side down, on a cutting board and cut each tail in half lengthwise. Remove the two halves of meat from each tail. Crack the claws, using a nutcracker or hammer, and gently remove the claw meat (the idea is to keep the claw meat intact). Discard the shells or save them for another use.

5. Process the egg in a food processor until light in color. Gradually drizzle in the oil, processing until it is well emulsified. Add ¼ cup of the roasted peaches, the remaining 2 tablespoons lemon juice, and the parsley, tarragon, and curry powder. Process until smooth.

6. In a large bowl, toss the lobster tails and claws with 2 tablespoons of the dressing. In another bowl, toss the mâche and frisée with the remaining dressing. Divide the greens among six chilled plates. Place a lobster tail and claw in the center of each plate. Divide the roasted peaches among the plates, and serve.

Shrimp Salad with Cilantro and Sweet Corn Salsa

SERVES 6

This is a summertime salad that's substantial enough for an entree. Thread the shrimp on bamboo skewers for a nice presentation.

---

2 cups sweet corn kernels, cooked

2 plum tomatoes, seeded and chopped

1 jalapeño pepper, seeded and minced

¼ cup chopped scallions, white parts only

4 tablespoons chopped cilantro

9 tablespoons extra virgin olive oil

3 teaspoons fresh lime juice

18 extra-large shrimp, tails on, peeled and deveined

1 head Boston lettuce, leaves separated

---

1. Preheat a grill or broiler.

2. In a mixing bowl, toss the corn, tomatoes, pepper, scallions, 3 tablespoons of the cilantro, 4 tablespoons of the olive oil, and 2 teaspoons of the lime juice. Set aside.

3. Toss the shrimp with 3 tablespoons of the olive oil, and grill until cooked through, about 2 minutes per side.

4. Combine the remaining 2 tablespoons olive oil, 1 teaspoon lime juice, and 1 tablespoon chopped cilantro in a bowl, and toss with the lettuce. Divide the lettuce among six plates and place three shrimp in the center of each. Spoon the salsa over the salad, and serve.

NOTE: The salsa may be made up to 2 hours in advance and refrigerated until ready to serve.

MEAT

Our most popular dinner entrees are some of the easiest to prepare. These recipes are straightforward and concentrate on enhancing a main ingredient, so they require the highest-quality meat. Find a butcher who can provide you with cuts of the same quality that a restaurant purveyor supplies. Ask where the meat came from and how it was handled. Settle for nothing but the best.

Many of these entrees require little advance preparation, which makes them the perfect choice for a weekday supper or for impromptu entertaining. A few require a little advance planning, but most can be done the day before and so are a good choice for more formal entertaining. With some dishes, you may want to add a simply prepared seasonal vegetable to the plate. Then sit back and enjoy the compliments you'll receive when serving these elegant, easy dishes.

Beef Tenderloin with Caramelized Onion Tart

This onion tart is wonderful with many dishes; here I've paired it with thin slices of filet mignon. Most of the preparation may be done in advance, so all you need to do at the last minute is to bake the tart and grill the meat. I often serve a smaller portion of this dish as a first course.

---

1 large egg	3 large sweet onions, peeled and
½ cup corn oil	thinly sliced
3 tablespoons Dijon mustard	2 teaspoons chopped thyme
1 tablespoon minced garlic	Six 7- to 8-ounce filets mignons,
1 tablespoon white wine vinegar	1½ inches thick
1 sheet Simple Puff Pastry	Salt and pepper
(page 33)	2 teaspoons chopped flat-leaf
¼ cup unsalted butter	parsley

---

1. Process the egg in a food processor or blender until light in color. Gradually drizzle in the oil, processing until it is well emulsified. Add the mustard, garlic, and vinegar, and process until smooth. Set aside.

2. Preheat the oven to 375°F.

3. Fit the puff pastry into a 9- or 10-inch tart pan with a removable bottom. Trim off the excess and line the bottom with pie weights. Bake the tart shell for 12 to 15 minutes, until just beginning to brown. Allow to cool completely.

4. Melt the butter in a large skillet. Add the onions and cook over low heat, stirring often, until soft and caramelized, about 15 minutes. Spread the onions in the cooled pastry shell. Sprinkle the thyme over the onions, and bake for 10 to 12 minutes, until the tips of the onions are just beginning to brown.

5. In the meantime, preheat a grill or broiler.

6. Season the filets to taste, and grill about 7 minutes per side for medium-rare (longer for medium to well-done, less for rare). Remove the filets from the grill and allow them to rest for a few minutes.

7. Drizzle the mustard sauce on six warmed plates. Slice the onion tart into six wedges, and place a wedge on each plate. Slice the filets into thin pieces and fan them out on each plate. Sprinkle with the parsley, and serve.

NOTE: The Dijon sauce may be made up to 48 hours in advance and rewarmed to room temperature just before serving. The tart shell may be baked (unfilled) and the onions caramelized up to 8 hours before serving. When you are ready to serve, fill the tart and bake it.

Sirloin Strip Steak with Stilton Crust

Strip steak is a tender cut of sirloin with the bone and tenderloin removed. We serve it over a bed of leeks with a creamy Stilton crust that's melted under the broiler just before serving.

¾ cup crumbled Stilton

4 ounces cream cheese, softened

2 tablespoons chopped flat-leaf parsley

¼ cup unsalted butter

6 leeks, white parts only, thoroughly washed, julienned

¼ cup Madeira

Six 8-ounce strip steaks, about 1½ inches thick

Salt and pepper

---

1. Combine the Stilton, cream cheese, and parsley in a food processor, and process until smooth. Set aside.

2. Melt the butter in a large skillet. Add the leeks and cook until softened, 6 to 8 minutes. Add the Madeira, flame if desired (remove the skillet from the heat, and standing as far back as possible, ignite the liquid with a long match; swirl the skillet around until the flame dies out), and reduce for 1 minute. Keep warm.

3. Preheat the broiler.

4. Season the steaks to taste, and broil for about 6 minutes per side for medium-rare. Spread the cheese mixture over one side of the steaks, and place them under the broiler for 1½ to 2 minutes, until the cheese is heated through and just beginning to form a brown crust (watch them carefully to avoid overbrowning).

5. Divide the leeks among six warmed plates, place a steak on each, and serve.

NOTE: The Stilton–cream cheese mixture may be made up to 48 hours in advance and refrigerated until ready to use. It's also delicious spread on toasted slices of baguette and then broiled.

NOTES FROM THE INN:
RESTAURANT REVIEWS

For me, reviewers are the scariest part of owning a restaurant. Give me a surprise inspection by the health department and I can sail through with flying colors. Customer with food allergies? No problem. Request for a steak that's "cooked through but not well done"? I will rise to the occasion (people make the most ambiguous requests about meat temperatures, but that's another story). Of course, most reviewers focus mainly on the food, but any restaurant includes many other aspects of the dining experience. Is the music too loud? Is the server efficient? Does the reviewer like the courses to follow swiftly or does she prefer to sip her wine between courses and chat? Is the fire too warm? Is the room too cold? Does she prefer the fresh country air or air conditioning? When you add up all the variables, it's amazing anyone ever gets a decent review.

Our reviews have always been very positive. The good news for me as the chef has been that the reviewers have always loved my food. The minor complaints have mainly been over the music. We play a "light jazz" mix of Ella Fitzgerald/Louis Armstrong-type music at dinner, and several reviewers hated it. They felt that classical music would provide a more refined background for our elegant food.

Our first review came the week we opened the restaurant. I had sent out press releases to the local papers and had interested a reviewer from a small city nearby. She arrived anonymously with two friends (they have since become two of our best customers), jotted down some notes, and then had Bob call me out of the kitchen to tell me how wonderful the meal was. We were ecstatic. She didn't even seem to notice that there were only four other people dining that night!

Her review came out early that week and we were inundated with phone calls. Of course, never having run the front of the house in a restaurant, Bob began enthusiastically taking reservations until we were completely overbooked. When the weekend came and the diners started rolling in, we were overwhelmed. Bob went down to our wine cellar, where we were storing wines for a chef friend of ours, and began opening bottles from his well-aged Bordeaux collection, pouring complimentary glasses of wine to soothe those waiting for tables. After a few glasses, the atmosphere changed dramatically from an angry mob to a house party. Some of our customers still talk about those wines and what a great night it was.

Of course, you never know when reviewers have been in the restaurant until after they've gone. For this reason, you have to assume that any guest or diner might be a reviewer or a freelance writer. Our policy is to treat every guest with the same attention to detail as if they were a restaurant reviewer—and then hope they like the music.

Rack of Lamb with Mint Pesto and Chèvre Crust

SERVES 6

Lamb and lobster are our guests' two favorite entrees, perhaps partly because they're dishes people don't often prepare at home. This simply-assembled rack of lamb is easy to prepare at home and great for entertaining. The racks are smothered with mint pesto and topped with goat cheese and bread crumbs. The ribs are set over goat cheese mashed potatoes for a beautiful effect.

2 cups mint leaves, plus 6 mint sprigs
1 teaspoon minced garlic
¼ cup plus 2 tablespoons extra virgin olive oil
6 red-skinned potatoes, peeled and diced

3 lamb racks (8 ribs per rack), chined and frenched (see Note)
10 ounces fresh goat cheese, crumbled
¼ cup corn bread crumbs
¼ cup unsalted butter

1. Preheat the oven to 450°F.

2. Combine the mint, garlic, and ¼ cup olive oil in a food processor, and process until smooth. Set aside.

3. Place the potatoes in a medium saucepan, add lightly salted water to cover, and bring to a boil. Simmer until fork-tender, 12 to 15 minutes.

4. In the meantime, slice the lamb racks in half and trim off any fat. Brush the remaining 2 tablespoons olive oil over the lamb, cover the bones with foil, and place the racks in a shallow roasting pan. Roast the lamb for 12 minutes for medium-rare (4 to 8 minutes longer for medium to well-done, 4 minutes less for rare). Remove the lamb from the oven and spread the mint pesto over it. Press 8 ounces of the goat cheese over the lamb, and then press the bread crumbs into the cheese. Roast for 5 minutes longer, until the crust is heated through and browned. Remove the foil and allow the lamb to rest for a few minutes.

5. Drain the potatoes, put them in a mixing bowl, and mash in the butter and the remaining 2 ounces goat cheese. Pass the mixture through a food mill or ricer until smooth.

6. Divide the potatoes among six warmed plates. Carefully slice between the lamb ribs with a sharp knife, and arrange the chops over the potatoes. Garnish with the mint sprigs, and serve.

NOTE: Ask your butcher to prepare the racks by removing the chine (a bone that connects the individual ribs) and by scraping the bones clean to within one inch of the meat ("frenching").

Lamb Tenderloin with Ginger Soy Glaze

SERVES 6

Lamb tenderloins are a boneless cut that can be quickly grilled to perfection. Here they are served over glazed carrots and leeks to intensify the ginger soy taste.

¼ cup soy sauce

2 teaspoons minced fresh ginger

2 tablespoons light brown sugar

1 teaspoon Dijon mustard

6 lamb tenderloins, about 4 ounces each

2 tablespoons sesame oil

6 carrots, julienned

6 leeks, white parts only, thoroughly washed, julienned

---

1. Combine the soy sauce, ginger, brown sugar, and mustard in a small saucepan and simmer until slightly thickened, 5 to 7 minutes.

2. Preheat a grill or broiler.

3. Grill the lamb on a grill or broiler pan for 1½ minutes per side for medium-rare (1 to 2 minutes longer for medium to well-done, ½ minute less for rare). Reserving 1 tablespoon of the glaze, brush the lamb with the remaining glaze and allow it to rest for a few minutes.

4. In the meantime, heat the sesame oil in a large skillet. Add the carrots and leeks and sauté until just beginning to soften, 3 to 4 minutes. Remove from the heat and stir in the reserved 1 tablespoon soy glaze.

5. Slice the tenderloins into thin pieces, and arrange them on six warmed plates. Divide the carrots and leeks among the six plates, and serve.

Veal Medallions with Acorn Squash Bread Pudding

SERVES 6

A delicious savory bread pudding accompanies tender veal in one of our guests' favorite autumn combinations. The bread pudding is an excellent side dish for a Thanksgiving dinner as well. Veal demi-glace may be purchased at specialty food stores, through mail-order catalogs, or via the Internet; it adds a rich flavor to sauces.

---

1 acorn squash
1 cup heavy cream
¼ cup packed light brown sugar
1 teaspoon ground cinnamon
¼ teaspoon ground cloves
2 teaspoons chopped thyme, plus
    6 thyme sprigs
½ cup milk
2 large eggs
2 large egg yolks

6 slices Simple Brioche Loaf
    (page 62) or challah, cut into
    1-inch cubes
2 tablespoons unsalted butter
1 shallot, minced
Twelve 3-ounce veal cutlets, about
    ½ inch thick
Salt and pepper
Flour for dredging
½ cup Madeira
2 tablespoons veal demi-glace

---

1. Preheat the oven to 350°F. Butter six small ramekins.

2. Cut the squash in half and discard the seeds. Place the squash, cut side down, in a glass baking dish and cover with foil. Bake until tender, about 1 hour. Allow to cool and then scrape out the flesh. Discard the rinds.

3. Bring the heavy cream just to a boil in a medium-size saucepan and remove from the heat. Stir in the brown sugar, cinnamon, cloves, and chopped thyme. Process the acorn squash and the milk in a food processor or blender until smooth. Whisk the squash mixture into the cream. In a large bowl, whisk together the eggs and egg yolks. Stir the squash mixture into the eggs. Fold in the bread cubes.

4. Divide the mixture among the prepared ramekins. Place the ramekins in a 9 × 13-inch glass baking dish, and add enough boiling water to come at least halfway up the sides of the ramekins. Bake for 15 to 20 minutes, until just firm and lightly browned. Remove from the oven and keep warm.

5. Melt the butter in a large skillet and add the shallots. Season the veal cutlets to taste, dredge them lightly in flour, and add them to the pan. Sear each side over medium-high heat for 2½ to 3 minutes, until

the cutlets are lightly browned but still pink in the center. Transfer them to a warm platter. Add the Madeira to the skillet, flame if desired (remove the skillet from the heat and standing as far back as possible, ignite the liquid with a long match; swirl the skillet around until the flame dies out), and reduce by half, scraping up any tiny bits of meat. Add the veal demi-glace and remove from the heat.

6. Place the bread puddings on six warmed dinner plates, and arrange two pieces of veal on each plate. Drizzle the sauce over the veal, garnish with the thyme sprigs, and serve.

Integral Sauces

Many of the sauces in these recipes are made with the meat's pan juices. They use the flavor of the meat as a base for other added flavors. This is a simple way of achieving a more complex taste without spending a lot of time preparing a separate sauce to enhance the dish.

To make an integral sauce, heat the pan until the remaining juices and bits of meat are completely reduced and beginning to turn golden brown, and skim off any excess fat. Add wine or stock and allow it to reduce, scraping up any bits from the bottom of the pan. (Always add wine or any alcohol off the heat, because a high flame could ignite the contents of the bottle and cause it to explode.) You may want to flame the pan if you're adding alcohol, although the process of reducing eliminates most of the alcohol anyway. The safest way to flame the pan is to remove it from the burner and ignite the liquid with a long match, standing as far back as possible. Then swirl the pan around until the flame dies out. Finally, add more stock to the pan as necessary to attain the desired consistency. There are several excellent veal and duck stock reductions available commercially, allowing you to add complexity to sauces without spending the large amount of time needed to prepare them at home.

Veal Chop with Ginger, Pear, and Pancetta

In this sauce, the sweet combination of pear and ginger is nicely balanced by the slightly salty pancetta.

---

6 slices pancetta, chopped into
　　1-inch pieces
3 tablespoons unsalted butter
Six 10-ounce veal chops, frenched
　　to the eye (bones scraped clean
　　up to the meat on top)
Salt and pepper
3 Bosc or Comice pears, cored and
　　thinly sliced

1 tablespoon minced shallots
2 teaspoons grated fresh ginger
¼ cup ginger liqueur or brandy
3 tablespoons veal demi-glace
　　(see page 142)
2 teaspoons chopped thyme

---

1. Preheat the oven to 450°F.

2. Sauté the pancetta in a large skillet over medium heat until crisp and brown, about 10 minutes. Drain on paper towels and set aside.

3. Melt 2 tablespoons of the butter in a large skillet. Season the veal chops to taste, and add them to the pan. Sauté over high heat until golden, about 5 minutes per side. Remove the chops and reserve the skillet. Place the chops on a baking sheet or shallow roasting pan, transfer to the oven, and roast for 8 minutes until medium-rare (longer for medium to well-done, less for rare).

4. In the meantime, melt the remaining 1 tablespoon butter in the same skillet. Add the pears and sauté over low heat until just beginning to soften, about 3 minutes. Add the shallots and ginger, and stir for 1 minute. Add the ginger liqueur, flame if desired (remove the skillet from the heat, and standing as far back as possible, ignite the liquid with a long match; swirl the skillet around until the flame dies out), and reduce by half. Stir in the veal demi-glace and pancetta, and remove from the heat. Stir in the thyme. Arrange a veal chop on each plate, spoon the pear ginger sauce over them, and serve.

Portobellos with Herbed Goat Cheese and Balsamic Glaze

SERVES 6

Some of our dinner guests have given up eating meat, but they are often happily surprised by the meaty quality of these portobello caps.

¼ cup balsamic vinegar

4 tablespoons extra virgin olive oil

1 teaspoon minced garlic

12 portobello mushroom caps, all
    approximately the same size

2 cups crumbled fresh goat cheese
    (about 12 ounces)

¼ cup chopped scallions, white
    parts only

3 teaspoons chopped flat-leaf
    parsley

¼ cup chopped calamata olives

3 plum tomatoes, seeded and
    chopped

---

1. Preheat a grill or broiler. Preheat the oven to 375°F. Lightly grease a baking sheet with solid vegetable shortening.

2. Simmer the balsamic vinegar in a small saucepan over low heat until slightly reduced and syrupy, about 5 minutes.

3. Combine 2 tablespoons of the olive oil and ½ teaspoon of the garlic, and brush it all over the mushrooms. Grill the mushrooms until they're just beginning to soften, 2 to 3 minutes per side. Place 6 mushroom caps, gill side up, on the prepared baking sheet. Combine the goat cheese, scallions, and parsley in a bowl, and divide among the six caps. Place one of the remaining caps, gill side down, on top of each filled one, forming a sandwich or stack. Bake for 5 minutes, until the center is heated through.

4. In the meantime, heat the remaining 2 tablespoons olive oil in a large skillet. Add the remaining ½ teaspoon garlic, the olives, and the tomatoes, and sauté for 2 minutes. Place a portobello stack on each of six warmed plates, and spoon the tomato mixture around each stack. Reheat the balsamic glaze if necessary, and drizzle it on top. Serve immediately.

Chicken Breasts with Roquefort and Walnuts

Sometimes guests request a chicken dish for a special party, and this stuffed chicken breast is what I usually suggest: a creamy Roquefort filling wrapped in thin chicken cutlets and coated with walnuts. It's easily prepared ahead of time, making it the perfect dish for serving to a crowd.

4 ounces cream cheese, softened	3 whole boneless, skinless chicken
4 ounces Roquefort, crumbled	breasts (about 1½ pounds)
1 teaspoon minced garlic	Flour for dredging
1 tablespoon chopped flat-leaf	2 large eggs, beaten
parsley	1½ cups ground walnuts

1. Preheat the oven to 350°F. Lightly grease a baking dish with solid vegetable shortening.

2. Combine the cream cheese, Roquefort, garlic, and parsley in a food processor, and process until smooth; set aside.

3. Place each chicken breast between two sheets of waxed paper and pound it with a rolling pin or the flat side of a chef's knife until it is about ¼ inch thick. Cut the flattened breasts in half. Divide the filling into 6 portions and roll each into a log about 3 inches long. Place a piece on each piece of chicken breast, and roll the chicken up to completely enclose the cheese, tucking in the ends.

4. Place the flour, eggs, and walnuts in separate shallow dishes. Dredge the chicken rolls lightly in the flour, then the egg, and finally the walnuts. Place the chicken rolls in the prepared baking dish, cover with foil, and bake for 10 minutes. Remove the foil and bake for 5 to 8 minutes longer, until cooked through. Allow the rolls to rest for a few minutes. Then slice each roll into four or five pieces, arrange them on warmed plates, and serve.

Chicken Breast with Provençal Herbs and Truffles

SERVES 6

This is one of my favorite dishes to make at home because my kitchen smells so wonderful while the chicken is roasting. Fresh herbs and slices of black truffle are tucked under the skin of the chicken breast, infusing the meat with their flavors and aromas. Egg noodles tossed with buttery chanterelles complete this rustic but flavorful dish.

---

4 teaspoons chopped flat-leaf
    parsley
2 teaspoons chopped thyme
1 teaspoon chopped rosemary
¼ teaspoon minced lavender
    (optional)
6 bone-in chicken breast halves
    (with skin)
1 black truffle, thinly sliced

½ cup Madeira
¼ cup Grand Marnier
½ cup unsalted butter, melted, plus
    3 tablespoons unsalted butter
1 bay leaf
½ pound egg noodles
1 shallot, peeled and minced
½ cup chopped chanterelles or other
    mushrooms

---

1. Preheat the oven to 375°F.

2. Combine 2 teaspoons of the parsley with the thyme, rosemary, and lavender, if using, in a small bowl. Gently lift the skin on each chicken breast and press the herbs into the meat. Divide the truffle slices among the six pieces and layer them under the skin. Replace the skin and stretch it slightly to secure the herbs and truffle slices. Place the chicken in a single layer in a roasting or braising pan with a cover. Pour the Madeira, Grand Marnier, and melted butter over the chicken. Place the bay leaf in the pan, and cover the pan. Bake for about 45 minutes, until the chicken is cooked through. Remove the cover, and preheat the broiler. Place the chicken breasts under the broiler to brown, 12 to 15 minutes. Allow the chicken to rest for a few minutes.

3. In the meantime, bring about 4 quarts of lightly salted water to a boil in a large saucepan. Add the noodles, cook for 8 minutes, and drain. Melt the 3 tablespoons butter in a large skillet. Add the shallots and mushrooms, and sauté until soft, about 2 minutes. Remove from the heat and stir in the noodles and the remaining 2 teaspoons parsley. Divide the noodles among six warmed plates. Place a piece of chicken on each plate, and serve.

Quail with Roasted Strawberry Chutney

Roasting fresh strawberries brings out their flavor, which is the perfect foil for the delicate taste of quail. Because the quail roast so quickly, they make an excellent choice for a last-minute meal.

---

12 semi-boneless quail (ask the butcher to prepare them)
Salt and pepper
2 cups strawberries, hulled and quartered
1 tablespoon unsalted butter, melted

¼ cup coarsely chopped sweet onion
3 tablespoons brown sugar
2 tablespoons Grand Marnier
1 teaspoon grated orange zest
½ teaspoon ground cinnamon
½ teaspoon ground ginger
1 tablespoon cider vinegar

---

1. Preheat the oven to 400°F.

2. Season the quail with salt and pepper to taste. Tie the legs of each quail together, and set the quail in a shallow roasting pan with the legs pointing up. Roast for 20 minutes.

3. In the meantime, combine the remaining ingredients in a medium bowl. Place the mixture in a shallow baking dish and roast alongside the quail for 10 to 12 minutes, until the strawberries are just softened.

4. Spoon the strawberry chutney around the quail and serve.

NOTES FROM THE INN: THE SUITES

I've always been driven to make improvements at the inn. After all, when *we* travel, I like to be at least as comfortable as when I'm at home, if not more so. So we're constantly reinvesting our income into making the inn more comfortable. Sometimes this means simple things, such as upgrading the robes or towels. Often it has meant major construction, like adding whirlpool tubs and fireplaces. The first suite was one of these major projects.

We initially opened the inn with six guest rooms, each with a private bath. Once our reputation grew, we realized that some of our clientele would appreciate a larger, more deluxe accommodation. So we began looking around the inn, trying to figure out where we could add a suite. By building a new staircase, using part of our living quarters, to the vaulted storage area on the third floor, guests could have a private entrance to the new suite. It meant removing the entire back wall and adding floor-to-ceiling windows and a half-moon window. For me, it meant the excitement of designing and furnishing a new space—a tedious and time-consuming process, but so rewarding when the whole thing comes together.

As a matter of fact, I have a recurring dream about the inn, in which I find rooms I never knew we had before. Sometimes I discover a hallway full of doors, filled with rooms waiting to be discovered. Other times, I discover a grand ballroom with hardwood floors and soaring ceilings. This dream is a little stressful, because I can't figure out how I'm going to get the painting done! I always feel a little disappointed when I wake up to realize that I won't need to audition a pianist to play the baby grand in the new ballroom.

The only real "addition" we've ever built was a second floor to our carriage house/garage. This is sort of a running joke with us, since so many inns call their garage a "carriage house"—but in our case, it's actually true. Although we keep our cars in it now, we discovered when we tore off the existing roof that the building really was designed for carriages. The date of the original construction, 1895, was carved into the huge ceiling beam, confirming its pre-automobile history. This second floor was originally added as a studio space for Bob. The initial design included French doors with a private deck, a full tiled bath, and a fireplace. But as I started looking around the property, it became the obvious choice for an additional suite. We would merely need to add a whirlpool tub—and, yes, redecorate—to make it a perfect hideaway. So we built Bob a new studio space, moved him out, and went to work. The Garden Gate and Palladian Suites are now our two most popular rooms.

We now have eight guest accommodations, which is about all we can handle without adding more staff. We have cleaning help, but Bob and I still do much of the day-to-day work. We still get to spend some time with our guests, particularly at breakfast. We keep the inn large enough to make it a viable business, but small enough to make it not *seem* like a business. Of course I do have one more project on my list, when I find the space. It's a ballroom with a baby grand piano. I'm willing to compromise, though—I'm planning to hire a painter.

Venison Medallions with Cranberries and Mascarpone

Venison tenderloins from New Zealand have a deep burgundy color and a unique rich taste. The tenderloin is a delicate cut and is best cooked briefly to preserve its tenderness. I usually serve game like venison in the colder months, so cranberries are the perfect complement.

---

6 tablespoons unsalted butter

1 shallot, chopped

2 cups cooked wild rice
   (about ½ cup uncooked)

3 venison tenderloins

Flour for dredging

½ cup dried cranberries

½ cup Madeira

¼ cup mascarpone

---

1. Melt 4 tablespoons of the butter in a large skillet and sauté the shallots until translucent, 3 to 4 minutes. Stir in the wild rice and cook until just warmed through. Remove from heat and keep warm.

2. Trim off the ends of the tenderloins and slice the remaining pieces into 2-inch-thick medallions. Pound each piece to flatten it slightly. Melt the remaining 2 tablespoons butter in a large skillet over high heat. Lightly dredge the medallions in the flour, and sauté them until browned but still rare in the center, about 2 minutes per side. Remove the medallions from the skillet and keep warm. Add the cranberries and Madeira to the skillet, flame if desired (remove the skillet from the heat, and standing as far back as possible, ignite the liquid with a long match; swirl the skillet around until the flame dies out), and cook for 30 seconds, scraping up any bits of meat. Remove the skillet from the heat and stir in the mascarpone until just melted.

3. Divide the rice and the medallions among six warmed plates. Spoon on the sauce, and serve.

NOTE: Wild rice actually isn't rice at all; it's the seed of a wild grass. To prepare the wild rice, simply bring 6 cups of lightly salted water to a boil and add ½ cup wild rice. Simmer the rice until all the water is absorbed and the rice is tender, about 1 hour. Some of the grains of rice will begin to split open, exposing the white centers. The rice may be cooked up to 48 hours in advance and refrigerated until ready to use. Reheat the rice briefly in boiling water or in a microwave.

Caramelized Duck Breast
with Wild Mushrooms

SERVES 6

Caramelizing duck breasts yields a crisp skin and perfectly cooked meat. The wild mushrooms add an interesting flavor and texture without increasing the inherent richness of the duck.

Six 8- to 10-ounce boneless duck
    breasts
Salt and pepper
6 tablespoons unsalted butter
1 teaspoon chopped shallot
1 pound fresh wild mushrooms
    (chanterelles, black trumpets,
    or others)

¼ cup Madeira or dry sherry
3 tablespoons duck or veal demi-
    glace (see page 142)
2 teaspoons chopped flat-leaf
    parsley

1. Heat two large skillets. Prick the skin of the duck breasts with a fork without piercing the meat, and season with salt and pepper. Place the breasts, skin side down, in the hot skillets. Sauté over medium heat, pricking the skins and draining off the excess fat every few minutes, until most of the fat is rendered and the skin is crisp and golden, about 10 minutes. Turn and cook on the other side for 4 minutes for medium-rare. Remove from the pan and keep warm.

2. In the meantime, melt 3 tablespoons of the butter in a large skillet. Add 1 tablespoon of the rendered duck fat. Add the shallots and mushrooms, and sauté over low heat until they are softened and most of the liquid is gone, 6 to 8 minutes. Add the Madeira, flame if desired (remove the skillet from the heat, and standing as far back as possible, ignite the liquid with a long match; swirl the skillet around until the flame dies out), and cook for 1 minute. Stir in the duck demi-glace and the remaining 3 tablespoons butter, and remove from the heat. Sprinkle the parsley over the mixture.

3. Slice the duck breasts, cutting downward through the skin with a very sharp knife, and serve with a mound of the mushrooms.

Rabbit Tenderloins with Pumpkin, Wild Rice, and Apricots

SERVES 6

Farm-raised rabbits have juicy white meat. The pumpkin stuffing requires some preparation and baking time, but it can be done ahead. The tenderloin is quickly pan-seared and glazed with apricots to complete the dish.

---

10 tablespoons unsalted butter	½ teaspoon chopped sage
1 teaspoon chopped shallot	2 teaspoons chopped flat-leaf
3 cups shredded fresh pumpkin	parsley
(see page 211)	2 cups half-and-half
½ cup dried apricots, finely chopped	2 tablespoons extra virgin olive oil
½ cup slivered almonds	12 rabbit loins, 2 to 3 ounces each
2 cups cooked wild rice	Salt and pepper
(about ½ cup uncooked;	6 apricots, peeled, pitted, and thinly
see Note, page 151)	sliced
2 cups corn bread stuffing	1 teaspoon sugar
2 teaspoons chopped thyme	½ cup apricot preserves

---

1. Preheat the oven to 350°F. Butter a 2½-quart glass baking pan or casserole dish.

2. Melt 6 tablespoons of the butter in a large skillet. Add the shallots and pumpkin, and stir to coat with the butter. Remove from the heat and pour the mixture into a large bowl. Stir in the dried apricots, almonds, wild rice, corn bread stuffing, thyme, sage, and parsley. Then stir in the half-and-half. Spoon the mixture into the prepared pan, dot the top with 2 tablespoons butter, and cover with foil. Bake for 20 minutes. Then remove the foil and bake for about 10 minutes longer, until golden and heated through.

3. Heat the olive oil in a large skillet. Season the rabbit loins and sauté until golden on all sides, about 4 minutes. Remove from the skillet and set aside to rest.

4. Melt the remaining 2 tablespoons butter in the same skillet, add the sliced apricots, and sprinkle with the sugar. Cook until just softened, about 2 minutes.

5. Heat the apricot preserves to just boiling in a small saucepan, and brush it on the rabbit loins. Spoon some pumpkin dressing onto each plate. Slice each rabbit loin into 5 pieces and arrange around the dressing. Spoon the warm apricots over the rabbit, and serve.

NOTE: The pumpkin dressing may be assembled up to 24 hours in advance and refrigerated.

Winter at the Inn Means . . .

Enjoying a slower pace as the busy foliage season comes to an end.

Spending more time in the kitchen developing new dishes.

Setting a fire for guests to enjoy while they partake of afternoon tea.

Being inundated with seed catalogs and carefully making selections.

Noticing that guests spend more time around the inn as the days get shorter and colder.

Listening to the farm reports about the severity of impending snowstorms.

Worrying about guests getting trapped in inclement weather.

Walking my dogs in freshly fallen snow.

Decorating for the holidays, and anticipating some time off when they're over.

Finalizing the New Year's Eve plans and coming up with menus.

Closing for January to refresh ourselves and the appearance of the inn.

Getting away briefly to somewhere warm and sunny.

Gearing up for the Valentine's Day weekend and bringing the sleeping inn back to life.

Growing weary of snowstorms and all the extra work they bring.

Using the last of the tomato sauce from the freezer, eager to start the first tomato plants indoors.

SEAFOOD

Seafood is overwhelmingly the most popular entree choice on our dinner menu. Since we're landlocked here in Pennsylvania, I have had to search out the best seafood purveyors and develop good relationships with them. My purveyors know that I won't settle for anything less than the freshest, highest-quality seafood, so they go to great lengths to ensure that I get it. In return, I make sure I let them know how much our guests appreciate that quality, so they get to share in the kudos we receive. If you want to learn about the quality of the seafood you're buying, begin by asking a lot of questions at the fish counter. How can you tell if a fish is really fresh? Where were these lobsters harvested? What makes one type of shrimp more expensive than another? The fishmonger's enthusiasm in answering these questions will give you a good sense of how passionate he or she is about selling quality fish. For these recipes, use only the best seafood as a starting point.

Jumbo Lump Crab Cakes with Almonds

During the à la carte days of the restaurant, we often ran out of these crab cakes early in the evening. The secret to their great flavor is really no secret at all—it's the excellent quality of the pure Chesapeake crabmeat being allowed to shine through. The crab is tossed with a lightly seasoned mayonnaise, then given a light coating of almonds and briefly sautéed.

3 large eggs	1 teaspoon Old Bay seasoning
1 cup corn oil	2 pounds jumbo lump crabmeat
Dash of Worcestershire sauce	Flour for dredging
1 teaspoon Dijon mustard	2 cups sliced almonds
2 tablespoons white wine vinegar	3 tablespoons unsalted butter
2 tablespoons chopped flat-leaf parsley	

1. Process 1 egg in a food processor until it is light in color. Gradually drizzle in the oil, processing until it is well emulsified. Add the Worcestershire, mustard, vinegar, parsley, and Old Bay, and process until combined.

2. Set aside ⅓ cup of the mayonnaise, and place the rest in a mixing bowl. Add the crabmeat, and toss gently to combine. Form the mixture into twelve cakes.

3. In a shallow bowl, whisk together the remaining 2 eggs. Place the flour and the almonds in separate shallow dishes. Dip each crab cake into flour, then egg, and finally almonds, coating both sides. Place the crab cakes on waxed paper.

4. Melt the butter in a large skillet. Add the crab cakes and sauté until golden brown and heated through, about 3 minutes per side. Drizzle the remaining mayonnaise over them, and serve.

NOTE: The mayonnaise may be made up to 48 hours in advance and refrigerated until ready to use.

Scallops with Saffron and Risotto Cakes

The slightly sticky quality of risotto makes it easy to form the little rice cakes that accompany this dish. A smaller portion makes an excellent first course.

3 cups Basic Chicken Stock (page 87)	6 thyme sprigs
1 small onion, quartered	3 cups cooked risotto (see page 40)
1 small carrot, chopped	8 tablespoons unsalted butter
1 celery stalk, chopped	18 jumbo scallops
Pinch of saffron threads	Flour for dusting
	2 tablespoons chopped dill

1. Combine the stock, onions, carrots, celery, saffron, and thyme sprigs in a medium saucepan and bring to a boil. Simmer until reduced by about two thirds, about 45 minutes. Strain and set aside.

2. Form the risotto into six cakes, each about 3 inches across. Melt 2 tablespoons of the butter in a large skillet. Add the risotto cakes and cook until golden and heated through, 2 to 3 minutes per side. Keep warm.

3. Melt 2 tablespoons of the butter in another large skillet. Lightly dust the scallops with flour, and sauté until golden, 3 to 4 minutes per side.

4. Reheat the saffron broth if necessary, and whisk in the remaining 4 tablespoons butter. Place a risotto cake in each of six warmed shallow bowls. Arrange three scallops in each of the bowls, and ladle the broth over them. Sprinkle with the chopped dill, and serve.

Shrimp with Lemon, Pesto, and Pine Nuts

Shrimp are sized according to how many will make up a pound. I use U-10 or U-12 shrimp (10 or 12 per pound) for this tasty dish. For an appetizer version, two shrimp is a reasonable portion size. Substitute tender spinach if sorrel is unavailable.

6 tablespoons unsalted butter	2 teaspoons minced lemon zest
1 clove garlic, minced	4 tablespoons basil pesto
30 jumbo shrimp, tails on, peeled	2 tablespoons extra virgin olive oil
and deveined	4 cups loosely packed sorrel or
½ cup white wine	baby spinach
1 tablespoon fresh lemon juice	½ cup pine nuts, toasted

1. Melt 2 tablespoons of the butter in a large skillet. Add the garlic and shrimp, and sauté until the shrimp are lightly browned, about 4 minutes. Add the wine and cook until completely evaporated, about 2 minutes. Sprinkle on the lemon juice and zest, and stir for 30 seconds. Remove the skillet from the heat, and stir in 2 tablespoons of the pesto and the remaining 4 tablespoons butter.

2. Heat the olive oil in a large skillet and add the sorrel. Sauté until just wilted, about 1½ minutes.

3. Divide the sorrel among six warmed plates. Arrange five shrimp around the sorrel, and dot the plates with the remaining 2 tablespoons pesto. Sprinkle the pine nuts over the shrimp, and serve.

Salmon with Basil Pesto and Polenta Crust

Our fixed menu offers an alternative entree choice, and I often use salmon because of its popularity. In this version, the salmon is broiled, then coated with fresh basil pesto and finished with a creamy corn bread crust.

---

2 cups half-and-half

½ cup yellow cornmeal

2 tablespoons mascarpone

¼ cup white wine

3 tablespoons fresh lemon juice

¼ cup unsalted butter

Six 6-ounce pieces of salmon fillet, each about 2 inches wide, skin removed

¼ cup basil pesto

2 tablespoons chopped flat-leaf parsley

---

1. Preheat the broiler. Bring the half-and-half to a boil in a medium saucepan, and lower the heat to a simmer. Gradually add the cornmeal, whisking constantly until it is completely incorporated. Using a wooden spoon, continue stirring and cooking until the mixture thickens and pulls away from the sides of the pan, 3 to 4 minutes. Remove the pan from the heat and stir in the mascarpone.

2. Simmer the white wine in a small saucepan until reduced to 2 to 3 tablespoons, then remove from the heat. Stir in the lemon juice and butter, and keep warm.

3. Broil the salmon fillets until cooked through, about 4 minutes per side (less if you like the center rare). Remove the salmon from the broiler and spread the basil pesto over the tops of the fillets. Spread the polenta evenly over the pesto, and return the fillets to the broiler to brown slightly (the polenta side should be up), 3 to 4 minutes.

4. Stir the parsley into the lemon butter sauce, and drizzle it around the fillets. Serve immediately.

NOTE: The polenta may be made up to 8 hours in advance and refrigerated until ready to use. Bring it to room temperature to make it more malleable.

Salmon Roulade with Garlic Potatoes

SERVES 6

Salmon is rolled around a creamy garlic potato filling here, and baked until lightly browned. Anchovies provide the exciting taste in the buttery lemon sauce.

3 large red-skinned potatoes, peeled and quartered	½ cup white wine
2 teaspoons minced garlic	6 oil-packed anchovy fillets (about ½ can)
¾ cup unsalted butter	3 tablespoons fresh lemon juice
Six 7-ounce pieces of salmon fillet, each about 1 inch wide, skin removed	2 tablespoons chopped chives

1. Preheat the oven to 375°F. Line a 9 × 13-inch baking dish with foil.

2. Place the potatoes in a medium saucepan, and add lightly salted water to cover. Bring to a boil, and cook until soft, about 20 minutes. Drain the potatoes and put them in a mixing bowl. Mash with 1½ teaspoons of the garlic and ¼ cup of the butter. Pass the potatoes through a food mill or ricer, then whip until smooth and fluffy.

3. Roll each salmon fillet into the shape of a donut, and affix the ends with a toothpick. Place them in the baking dish. Fill the center of each piece with the potatoes. Cover with foil and bake for 10 minutes. Remove the foil and bake until the potatoes are golden brown, about 5 minutes longer.

4. In the meantime, combine the wine, anchovies, and remaining ½ teaspoon garlic in a small saucepan. Cook, stirring often, until the anchovies are dissolved and only a few tablespoons of liquid remain. Remove from the heat and whisk in the lemon juice and the remaining ½ cup butter.

5. Using a spatula, transfer the salmon fillets to warmed plates. Carefully twist out the toothpick, leaving the roll intact. Drizzle the anchovy sauce over the rolls, sprinkle with the chives, and serve.

NOTE: The potatoes may be made up to 8 hours in advance and refrigerated until ready to use.

Seafood Pot Pie with Saffron and Dill

SERVES 6

This luscious version of a pot pie combines shrimp, scallops, and crab in a saffron-scented dill cream. The pastry top puffs as the pot pie bakes, making a dramatic presentation. Our guests always "ooo" and "aahh" when this dish is set before them, still bubbling from the oven.

¼ cup unsalted butter

1 shallot, minced

2 small carrots, finely chopped

18 large shrimp, peeled and deveined

18 medium dry sea scallops

2 tablespoons all-purpose flour

½ cup white wine

1 cup heavy cream

2 cups half-and-half

Pinch of saffron threads

½ teaspoon salt

½ teaspoon white pepper

2 teaspoons chopped dill

2 teaspoons fresh lemon juice

1 pound jumbo lump crabmeat

Two 10 × 13-inch sheets Simple Puff Pastry (page 33)

1 large egg

---

1. Preheat the oven to 375°F. Butter six individual tall soufflé cups.

2. Melt the butter in a large skillet. Add the shallots and carrots, and sauté for about 1 minute. Add the shrimp and scallops and sauté, stirring constantly, for 1 minute. Sprinkle the flour over all and cook for 30 seconds. Add the wine and cook for 1 minute. Add the heavy cream and cook for 1 minute. Stir in the half-and-half, saffron, salt, and white pepper, and remove from the heat. Stir in the dill and lemon juice. Gently fold in the crabmeat. Divide the mixture among the prepared soufflé cups.

3. Cut out six pastry circles large enough to cover the soufflé cups and extend ½ inch over the edge. Lay the pastry over each cup, pressing the edges to seal them. Whisk the egg with a little water, and brush the egg wash over the pastry tops. Bake for 12 to 15 minutes, until the pastry tops are puffed and golden and the mixture is just beginning to bubble over. Allow to cool for a few minutes before serving.

Lobster Tarts with Leeks and Dill Cream

Fresh lobster is baked in a puff pastry shell and finished with a rich cream in this elegant dish.

---

2 sheets Simple Puff Pastry (page 33)	3 cups coarsely chopped steamed lobster meat (from about six 1¼-pound lobsters)
1¼ cups white wine	1 tablespoon all-purpose flour
1 shallot, coarsely chopped	2 tablespoons fresh lemon juice
1 cup heavy cream	¼ cup dill, chopped
½ cup unsalted butter	
3 leeks, white parts only, thoroughly washed, chopped	

---

1. Preheat the oven to 375°F.

2. Butter six individual tart pans, and line them with the puff pastry, trimming off any excess. Line the pans with pie weights, and bake for 12 to 15 minutes, until the pastry is just beginning to brown. Allow to cool completely.

3. Combine 1 cup of the wine and the shallots in a medium saucepan, and bring to a boil. Simmer until about 3 tablespoons of liquid remain, 8 to 10 minutes. Remove the shallots with a slotted spoon and add the cream. Reduce on low heat until slightly thickened, about 10 minutes.

4. In the meantime, melt ¼ cup of the butter in a large skillet. Add the leeks and the lobster, and sprinkle with the flour. Sauté until the leeks begin to soften, about 2 minutes. Stir in the lemon juice and the remaining ¼ cup wine, and cook for 30 seconds. Divide the lobster mixture among the tart shells, and bake for 8 minutes.

5. Whisk the remaining ¼ cup butter into the cream, and stir in the dill. Drizzle the sauce over the tarts, and serve.

Lobster with Fingerling Potatoes
and Citrus Sauce

SERVES 6

This simple preparation gets rave reviews from guests because the lobster is always so tender. A pinwheel of roasted fingerlings is set on each warmed plate, topped with the lobster, and drizzled with a concentrated citrus butter. The lobsters are steamed just long enough so the meat can be removed from the shells, then plunged into ice water to stop the cooking. Once the meat is removed from the shell, it may be refrigerated for up to 24 hours in advance, making this dish a perfect choice for entertaining.

6 live lobsters, 1½ pounds each	6 thyme sprigs
2 cups Basic Chicken Stock	12 fingerling potatoes
(page 87)	¼ cup chopped flat-leaf parsley
1 shallot, chopped	1 tablespoon extra virgin olive oil
½ cup fresh lemon juice	½ cup unsalted butter
½ cup fresh orange juice	

1. Fill a lobster pot or a large stockpot with 2 inches of water and bring to a boil. Plunge the lobsters into the boiling water, then cover and cook until they've just turned red, about 8 minutes. Remove the lobsters from the pot and immediately submerge them in ice water. Allow to cool.

2. Pull off the lobster claws and tails, and discard the bodies or reserve them for other use. Place the tails, hard side down, on a cutting board and cut each tail in half lengthwise. Remove the two halves of meat from each tail. Using a nutcracker or hammer, crack the claws and gently remove the claw meat (try to keep the claw meat intact). Discard the shells or save them for another use.

3. Combine the stock, shallots, ¼ cup of the lemon juice, the orange juice, and the thyme sprigs in a medium saucepan and bring to a boil. Simmer until reduced by three quarters 20 to 30 minutes. Allow to cool, then strain the liquid into a clean saucepan and discard the solids.

4. Slice the fingerling potatoes into thin discs. Place the potatoes in a medium skillet and add lightly salted water just to cover. Sprinkle with the salt and simmer until the potatoes are just tender, about 3 minutes. Drain and allow to cool.

5. Preheat the oven to 375°F. Line two 9 × 13-inch baking pans with foil, and butter them lightly.

6. Arrange the lobster tails, in pairs, in one of the baking pans. Twine the tails around each other. Top each pair of tails with two claws. Sprinkle with the parsley and the remaining ¼ cup lemon juice, and set aside.

7. In the second baking pan, arrange the potatoes in six 4-inch-wide pinwheels of overlapping slices. Drizzle the olive oil over the potatoes.

8. Place both pans in the oven and roast for 8 minutes, until the lobster is just heated through and the potatoes are beginning to turn golden.

9. Meanwhile, heat the citrus sauce in a saucepan and whisk in the butter, in bits, until combined.

10. Using a large spatula, place a potato round on each of six warmed plates. Place a lobster on top of each potato round, drizzle with the warm sauce, and serve.

LOBSTER BASICS

Many of our guests love lobster, so we've served a lot of them at the inn. We exclusively use what we think is the best lobster available, *Homarus americanus*, or the American lobster, shipped to us live from the cold coastal waters of Maine. Lobster is naturally low in fat and has about half the calories of an equal portion of skinless chicken. Because it arrives live, lobster is one of the few seafood items that's guaranteed to be fresh. Here are some tips for preparing lobster at home.

• Purchase only live lobsters—some part of the lobster should be moving. You can't salvage a lobster once it's dead. The meat of dead lobsters has a foul odor and flavor when cooked.

• It takes about 4 pounds of live lobster to get about 1 pound of meat during the winter months, when lobsters are most full of meat. In late summer, when the lobsters shed their shells and become soft, it may take more lobsters to get this much meat. One pound of lobster meat is the equivalent of about 2 cups.

• A Maine lobster's favorite meal is another Maine lobster, so no wonder it tastes so good! This is one reason why the claws of lobsters are banded (the other is for ease of handling). It is not necessary to remove the bands before steaming.

• Lobsters packed in ice will last at least 1 day. Lobsters kept in the refrigerator should be covered with a damp towel and will typically last up to 12 hours. Do not store lobsters in fresh water or in plastic bags—they will die.

• Large lobsters are just as tender as smaller ones when properly cooked. It takes 4 to 7 years for a lobster to reach 1 pound, so age has little to do with tenderness.

Lobster Fricassee with Corn and Chive Pancakes

SERVES 6

Sweet summertime corn enlivens these little pancakes, which taste almost like fritters.

1 cup yellow cornmeal	1 cup corn kernels, fresh or frozen
1 cup plus 1 tablespoon all-purpose flour	4 tablespoons chopped chives
1 teaspoon baking soda	Corn oil for frying
½ teaspoon salt	1 teaspoon minced shallots
1 cup buttermilk	3 cups coarsely chopped steamed
½ cup milk	lobster meat (from about six
1 large egg	1¼-pound lobsters)
¼ cup unsalted butter, melted, plus	2 tablespoons fresh lemon juice
3 tablespoons unsalted butter	¼ cup white wine
	½ cup heavy cream

1. Combine the cornmeal, 1 cup flour, baking soda, and salt in a large bowl. In another bowl, whisk together the buttermilk, milk, egg, and melted butter. Stir this into the dry ingredients until just combined. Fold in the corn and 3 tablespoons of the chives.

2. Heat about 1 inch corn oil in a large skillet. Add the batter, a tablespoon at a time, forming about six small pancakes. Fry until the edges begin to brown, about 1 minute, then carefully turn and fry until cooked through, about 1 minute longer. Remove the pancakes with a slotted spoon, drain on paper towels, and keep warm. Repeat this process until eighteen pancakes are completed.

3. Melt the 3 tablespoons butter in a large skillet. Add the shallots and lobster, and cook for 1 minute. Sprinkle with the remaining 1 tablespoon flour, and cook for 1 minute longer. Add the lemon juice and white wine, and cook until most of the liquid has been absorbed, about 1 minute. Stir in the cream and cook until slightly thickened, about 2 minutes. Arrange three pancakes on each warmed plate, and divide the lobster among the plates. Sprinkle with the remaining 1 tablespoon chives, and serve.

NOTE: The pancakes may be made up to 8 hours in advance; reheat and recrisp for a few minutes in a 400°F oven just before serving.

NOTES FROM THE INN:
THE FURNITURE MAKER

The commercial kitchen was only one of the expenses of opening the restaurant—we needed to furnish the dining room as well. While photographing one day, Bob met a young carpenter, an Old Order Mennonite (the strictest group of Mennonites) who made oak tables and Windsor chairs by hand (Old Order Mennonites do not use cars, electricity, or other modern conveniences). I checked the legal pad budget to see how much I had allocated for the furniture. We were getting close to the end of construction and the unexpected extra costs were piling up.

We arranged to meet the young man at his woodworking shop, where we found him at work, hand-finishing a beautiful pencil post bed. We selected the tables and chairs we liked from among his samples and asked for a quote. It was above my budget. I would have to look elsewhere for less expensive and perhaps less beautiful furniture.

"What's it going to take for you to buy these chairs?" the carpenter whispered to me. I explained that I loved the chairs but I could spend only the amount I had budgeted. "Well, I can't have anyone else's chairs in Churchtown," he said, and he thrust out his hand to make the deal official. He hastily drew up a sales slip with a description of the items at the reduced prices. Then to our absolute amazement, he opened a cabinet, pulled out a drawer with a copy machine hidden in it, and copied the bill of sale for us. It seems that besides being willing to negotiate pricing, he had decided to be flexible about the no-electricity dictate of his church. Perhaps the copier was merely regarded as a necessary evil.

We reviewed the paperwork and were pleased to discover that the price included local delivery as well. On a snowy March day, he arrived at the inn in a horse-drawn wagon piled high with our tables and chairs. They were beautiful and have remained so even with all the wear and tear over the years. Each time I show guests through the dining room, I'm struck by how the gleam of sunlight reflects off the satiny patina, and I remember how lucky we are to live among such talented, enigmatic, and thankfully sometimes flexible people.

TEATIME TREATS

Afternoon tea has a special role at the inn, and our teatime treats are among my most requested recipes. Guests often tell me that some of our cookies are now part of their holiday baking traditions. They're also a way for guests to take a little of the inn home to their families. These recipes provide a sweet solution, whether you're looking for an elegant dessert to complete a dinner party menu or just want to welcome your family home with a freshly baked treat.

Strawberry Mascarpone Meringues

SERVES 6

The wonderful macaroons found in France's finest bakeries inspired this version of individual strawberry tarts. The meringue cookie serves as the base for the creamy filling and fresh strawberries.

¼ cup hazelnuts, finely ground	¼ cup heavy cream
1 cup confectioners' sugar	2 tablespoons granulated sugar
2 large egg whites	¼ cup strawberry jelly or jam
¼ cup mascarpone	18 whole strawberries, hulled

1. Preheat the oven to 450°F. Line a large baking sheet with parchment paper, and butter it thoroughly.

2. Combine the hazelnuts and ¾ cup of the confectioners' sugar in a food processor or blender, and process until well mixed. In a bowl, beat the egg whites with an electric mixer until frothy. With the mixer running, gradually add the remaining ¼ cup confectioners' sugar. Beat until the egg whites are stiff but not dry. Gently fold the hazelnut mixture into the egg whites until combined. Transfer the mixture to a pastry bag with a ½-inch fluted tip. Pipe out six rings, each approximately 3 inches across and ¾ inch high, on the prepared baking sheet. Then pipe more batter to fill the centers, and smooth it out to create a flat bottom to hold the filling.

3. Lower the oven temperature to 300°F, place the baking sheet in the oven, and bake for 7 to 10 minutes, until the meringues look dry and crisp and are just beginning to brown (they will be soft on the inside). Immediately transfer the meringues to a wire rack and allow to cool completely before filling.

4. Combine the mascarpone, cream, and granulated sugar in the bowl of an electric mixer and beat until the mixture forms soft peaks. Refrigerate until ready to serve.

5. Heat the jelly in a small saucepan until just melted. Dip each strawberry into the jelly and then place it upright on waxed paper to set, about 5 minutes. When you are ready to serve them, divide the whipped cream among the centers of the six meringues, and set three strawberries on top of each one.

NOTE: The unfilled meringues may be made up to 2 days in advance and stored in an airtight container. The tarts may be assembled within 1 hour of serving; refrigerate until ready to serve.

Chocolate Chocolate Chips

MAKES 16 COOKIES

These rich chocolate cookies have a fudgelike center that's studded with chocolate chips. The cookies will still be slightly soft when removed from the oven, but they will firm up as they cool.

½ cup unsalted butter, softened
¼ cup packed light brown sugar
1 cup granulated sugar
1 large egg
1¼ cups all-purpose flour
½ teaspoon baking soda

½ teaspoon salt
¼ cup Dutch-process cocoa powder
2 tablespoons milk
3 ounces semisweet chocolate chips

---

1. Preheat the oven to 350°F. Lightly grease a cookie sheet with solid vegetable shortening.

2. In a large mixing bowl, combine the butter, brown sugar, and ¾ cup of the granulated sugar. Beat with an electric mixer until fluffy. Then beat in the egg. In another bowl, whisk together the flour, baking soda, salt, and cocoa powder. Beat the dry mixture into the butter mixture until just combined. Add the milk and mix briefly until combined. Stir in the chocolate chips.

3. Form the dough into sixteen balls, each about the size of a walnut (if the dough is too sticky, add a little extra flour). Place the remaining ¼ cup granulated sugar in a shallow bowl, and roll each ball in the sugar. Place on the prepared cookie sheet, and bake for 10 to 12 minutes, until the tops just begin to show cracks. Cool the cookies on wire racks.

Molasses Cookies

These cookies have a soft, chewy center and a subtle ginger scent.

½ cup unsalted butter, softened	½ teaspoon baking soda
¼ cup packed light brown sugar	½ teaspoon salt
1 cup granulated sugar	2 teaspoons ground ginger
¼ cup molasses	1 teaspoon ground cinnamon
1 large egg	¼ teaspoon ground cloves
1⅔ cups all-purpose flour	

1. Preheat the oven to 350°F. Lightly grease a cookie sheet with solid vegetable shortening.

2. In a large mixing bowl, combine the butter, brown sugar, and ¾ cup of the granulated sugar. Beat with an electric mixer until fluffy. Then beat in the molasses and egg. In another bowl, whisk together the flour, baking soda, salt, ginger, cinnamon, and cloves. Beat the dry mixture into the butter mixture until just combined.

3. Form the dough into sixteen balls, each about the size of a walnut (if the dough is too sticky, add a little extra flour). Pour the remaining ¼ cup granulated sugar into a shallow bowl, and roll each ball in the sugar. Place them on the prepared cookie sheet, and bake for 10 to 12 minutes, until the tops just begin to show cracks. Cool the cookies on wire racks.

NOTE: You can store these cookies in an airtight container for up to 3 days.

Pumpkin Raisin Squares

MAKES 16 SQUARES

These are dense little squares that concentrate flavor in every delicious bite. The icing is a creamy finishing touch.

---

6 tablespoons unsalted butter, softened

⅔ cup packed light brown sugar

1 large egg

½ cup canned pumpkin puree

½ cup all-purpose flour

½ teaspoon baking soda

½ teaspoon salt

¾ teaspoon ground cinnamon

½ teaspoon ground ginger

¼ teaspoon ground nutmeg

¼ teaspoon ground cloves

½ cup raisins

2 tablespoons cream cheese, softened

1 cup confectioners' sugar

---

1. Preheat the oven to 350°F, and butter an 8 × 8-inch baking pan.

2. In a large mixing bowl, beat 4 tablespoons of the butter with the brown sugar until fluffy. Beat in the egg and pumpkin. In another bowl, whisk together the flour, baking soda, salt, cinnamon, ginger, nutmeg, and cloves. Beat the dry mixture into the butter mixture until just combined. Then stir in the raisins. Spread the mixture in the prepared pan, and bake for 20 to 25 minutes, until a toothpick inserted into the center comes out clean. Allow it to cool slightly in the pan, then invert the pan onto a rack and cool completely.

3. Blend the remaining 2 tablespoons butter, the cream cheese, and confectioners' sugar in a small bowl until smooth (add a little hot water if necessary to bring to a spreading consistency). Spread the icing over the cooled cake and allow it to set up, about 10 minutes. Cut into sixteen squares.

VARIATION: Add ¼ cup chopped pecans or walnuts.

NOTE: The squares, without icing, may be stored in an airtight container for up to 3 days.

Teatime at the Inn

When we first opened the inn, I had never been to an afternoon tea—but I liked the sound of it so much that I included it in our list of amenities. Our version of afternoon tea is an informal gathering, enjoyed in the common areas with other guests or taken on trays to the privacy of guests' rooms or suites. In cooler weather, we serve a variety of hot teas to enjoy fireside. During the warmer months, guests might enjoy iced tea in the gardens. The array of offerings varies according to the season, but it always includes three or four baked goods, such as cookies and scones, and some savory finger sandwiches or cheeses. In February I might add chocolate-covered strawberries. In August I might wrap sweet melon in prosciutto. I change what I make each day to keep things interesting for me and for our guests, but some of the items have become such favorites that I include them often.

Since we opened, I've attended some formal afternoon tea parties and have been delighted to see how close our version is, except for the individual service. I think our informal approach works well for our guests, who might not enjoy the formality and structure of table service. I like the idea of our guests arriving back at the inn after a day of touring or shopping and being greeted with the aroma of freshly baked scones or cookies. Some guests arrive promptly at four P.M. just so they can enjoy the tea. They often take a few extra cookies upstairs for later. Afternoon tea is one of the amenities that guests most often mention in their positive comments about the inn.

Not all inns serve afternoon tea. Some inns host an evening wine-tasting. Others might offer guests a glass of sherry before dinner. Some inns don't feel compelled to offer any of these. It's part of the many individual decisions that make up the overall feeling of an inn. For us, afternoon tea is an important part of the personal warmth we offer our guests. It speaks well for us. "Welcome back," we're saying. "Help yourself to something wonderful to eat. Why not sit down and relax a while?" In essence, it's hospitality at its best.

Ladyfingers

4 large eggs, separated
½ cup granulated sugar
½ teaspoon vanilla extract

½ teaspoon salt
1 cup all-purpose flour
Confectioners' sugar, for dusting

1. Preheat the oven to 350°F. Butter two baking sheets, line them with parchment paper, and butter the parchment.

2. In a large bowl, beat the egg yolks and granulated sugar with an electric mixer until fluffy. Add the vanilla and whisk just to combine. In another bowl, beat the egg whites and salt until they form stiff peaks. Fold the whites into the egg yolk mixture. Add the flour in three separate additions, stirring until combined.

3. Spoon the batter into a pastry bag with a plain end. Pipe 3-inch-long cookies onto the prepared baking sheets, and dust them with confectioners' sugar. Bake for 12 to 15 minutes, until golden. Cool completely on wire racks.

NOTE: Ladyfingers may be made up to 48 hours in advance and stored in an airtight container.

Pecan Shortbread Bars

A buttery shortbread crust is baked with a pecan–cream cheese topping in this popular teatime treat.

---

1 cup all-purpose flour	3 tablespoons granulated sugar
¼ cup confectioners' sugar	1 large egg yolk
½ cup cold unsalted butter	1 teaspoon vanilla extract
4 ounces cream cheese, softened	1 cup chopped pecans

---

1. Preheat the oven to 350°F. Lightly grease an 8 × 8-inch baking pan with solid shortening.

2. Combine the flour and confectioners' sugar in a food processor. Add the butter, in bits, and process until crumbly. Press the mixture into the bottom of the prepared pan and bake for 15 minutes.

3. In the meantime, combine the cream cheese and granulated sugar in a bowl, and beat with an electric mixer until smooth. Beat in the egg yolk and vanilla. Stir in the pecans.

4. Spread the cream cheese mixture evenly over the baked crust. Bake for 8 to 10 minutes, until the topping is set. Cool in the pan, and cut into bars.

NOTE: These bars may be prepared up to 24 hours in advance and stored in an airtight container.

Almond Palmiers

MAKES 24 COOKIES

Palmiers are called the queen of French cookies, but the fact that they're so easy to make may dispel some of the mystique! My guests often request that I make this almond version for tea.

---

1 recipe Simple Puff Pastry (page 33)
4 ounces almond paste
1 cup sugar

---

1. Roll the dough out to form an 8 × 10-inch rectangle. Spread the almond paste over the dough, and sprinkle with ½ cup of the sugar. Fold in thirds (like a business letter), then rotate the dough so the top flap is to your right. Roll out the dough to form an 8 × 10-inch rectangle, sprinkle with the remaining ½ cup sugar, and again fold in thirds. Wrap in plastic wrap and refrigerate for 30 minutes.

2. Preheat the oven to 450°F.

3. Roll the dough again to form an 8 × 10-inch rectangle. Fold the two long sides to meet at the center, then fold them again (this creates the classic butterfly shape of the cookies). Slice the dough into twenty-four pieces, and place them on a baking sheet lined with parchment paper. Bake for 6 minutes, until the bottoms are caramelized. Turn the cookies and bake for 4 minutes longer, until golden. Cool on wire racks.

Easy Additions to a Tea Buffet

• Toast thin white bread and spread it with a mixture of butter and cinnamon sugar. Cut into wedges or use tiny cookie cutters to make decorative shapes.

• Spread a slice of white bread with butter and top with thinly sliced smoked salmon, salami, cucumbers, or radishes. Top with another piece of buttered bread and roll out flat with a rolling pin. Trim off the crusts and cut into triangles to serve as savory sandwiches.

• Slice a thin piece of pound cake and top with fruit preserves and shredded coconut. Place another thin slice on top and cut into four pieces.

• Cut up chunks of fresh melon and skewer them on toothpicks, alternating with grapes or strawberries.

• Split ladyfingers in half lengthwise and fill with whipped cream and raspberries, blueberries, or slices of fresh strawberries.

• Skewer chunks of Brie and pear together on toothpicks.

• Cut thin slices of pumpkin or zucchini bread, spread with cream cheese, and top with another thin slice. Cut into four pieces.

• Make a chocolate ganache fondue with melted chocolate and heavy cream, and skewer strawberries for dipping.

• Wrap blanched asparagus spears in thinly sliced prosciutto.

• Toast thin slices of baguette and top each with a slice of plum tomato and a thin slice of mozzarella. Serve cold or broil briefly until the cheese is melted.

• Spread a flour tortilla with cream cheese, horseradish, and thinly sliced roast beef or baby spinach. Roll up tightly, and slice into 1-inch pieces.

Apricot Coconut Almond Bars

MAKES 16 BARS

Apricot preserves are the tasty filling for these buttery squares.

---

2 cups all-purpose flour
½ cup sugar
¾ cup cold unsalted butter, cut into
    ¼-inch pieces
¼ teaspoon salt

½ cup sliced almonds
1¼ cups apricot preserves
    (12-ounce jar)
½ cup sweetened shredded
    coconut

---

1. Preheat the oven to 350°F. Butter an 8 × 8-inch baking pan.

2. Combine the flour, sugar, butter, and salt in a food processor, and process until crumbly. Stir in the almonds and reserve ¾ cup of the mixture. Press the remaining mixture into the prepared pan. Spread the apricot preserves and then the coconut over the crust. Top with the reserved crumbs. Bake for 30 to 35 minutes, until the preserves begin to bubble through the crumbs. Cool completely in the pan, then cut into sixteen bars.

NOTE: These bars may be made up to 24 hours in advance and stored in an airtight container.

Wild Blueberry Scones

MAKES 24 SCONES

Warm-from-the-oven scones might just be the quintessential teatime treat. Serve them with sweetened whipped cream, lemon curd, or fresh preserves. I most often make these scones with wild blueberries, but you might want to try a plain version or to add raisins or currants instead. This dough may be frozen as wedges and the scones baked as needed.

3 cups all-purpose flour	¾ cup buttermilk
½ cup granulated sugar	2 cups wild blueberries, frozen
1 tablespoon baking powder	3 tablespoons heavy cream
1 teaspoon baking soda	1 tablespoon sanding (decorative)
½ teaspoon salt	sugar
½ cup unsalted butter	

1. Preheat the oven to 350°F. Lightly grease a baking sheet with solid shortening.

2. Combine the flour, granulated sugar, baking powder, baking soda, and salt in a food processor. Add the butter in bits and process until crumbly. Turn the mixture into a large bowl, and stir in the buttermilk until just combined. Turn the dough onto a lightly floured work surface and fold in the frozen blueberries by hand. Divide the dough in half and form each half into a ball. Press the balls out to form 8-inch circles. Cut each circle into twelve wedges. Brush the tops with a little heavy cream, and sprinkle with sanding sugar. Place them on the prepared baking sheet and bake for 20 to 25 minutes, until golden. Cool slightly on wire racks.

NOTE: Using frozen blueberries prevents the berries from "bleeding" and turning the dough blue.

Wild Blueberries

You might have noticed that long after the days of our coastal Maine inn, I still use wild Maine blueberries in a lot of my recipes. Although we grow our own blueberries and take advantage of the cultivated blueberry harvest all summer long, nothing replaces the delicate flavor and size of the Maine berries. Every year we plan a trip to Maine in early August to take advantage of the brief wild blueberry harvest. We arrive in the barrens of Washington County and fill our coolers with quarts of fresh berries to bring home to use and to freeze. All winter long our guests know this trip was worthwhile when they reap the tasty benefits in freshly baked scones and other dishes.

Chocolate Chip Madeleines

MAKES 24 COOKIES

These cookies require a madeleine mold to create their signature shell-like shape. I use a non-stick mold to make it easier to dislodge the baked cookies.

½ cup unsalted butter	1 cup all-purpose flour
3 large eggs	½ teaspoon baking powder
⅔ cup sugar	¼ teaspoon salt
1 teaspoon vanilla extract	½ cup mini chocolate chips

1. Melt the butter in a small saucepan over medium heat and continue heating until it is just golden brown, 4 to 5 minutes. Allow to cool slightly.

2. In a large bowl, beat the eggs and sugar with an electric mixer until the mixture is lemony and forms ribbons when the beaters are lifted, about 5 minutes. Beat in the vanilla. In another bowl, whisk together the flour, baking powder, and salt. Gently fold the dry mixture into the egg mixture until just combined. Fold in the browned butter and the chocolate chips. Cover and refrigerate for 20 minutes.

3. Preheat the oven to 375°F. Generously grease two 12-mold madeleine pans with solid shortening.

4. Drop a tablespoon of the batter into the center of each mold, and bake for 12 to 15 minutes, until puffed and golden. Remove the pans and immediately invert them over a countertop covered with waxed paper; rap the pans if necessary to dislodge the cookies. Cool on wire racks.

VARIATION: Omit the chocolate chips and add ½ teaspoon lemon extract and 1 tablespoon poppy seeds.

NOTE: Don't smooth out the batter in the madeleine molds; allowing it to spread while baking achieves the cookies' traditional slightly humped shape.

These cookies may be made up to 1 day ahead and stored in airtight containers. However, they are best served just after cooling.

Oatmeal Chocolate Chip Cookies

MAKES 24 COOKIES

These cookies will taste great even after several days, but odds are they won't last that long.

½ cup unsalted butter, softened

½ cup packed light brown sugar

½ cup granulated sugar

1 large egg

2 teaspoons vanilla extract

2 tablespoons milk

1¼ cups all-purpose flour

½ teaspoon salt

½ teaspoon baking soda

1 cup old-fashioned oatmeal
   (rolled oats)

6 ounces semisweet chocolate chips

---

1. Preheat the oven to 350°F. Lightly grease a baking sheet with solid shortening.

2. In a large bowl, beat the butter, brown sugar, and granulated sugar with an electric mixer until fluffy. Beat in the egg, vanilla, and milk. In another bowl, whisk together the flour, salt, and baking soda. Beat the dry mixture into the butter mixture until just combined. Stir in the oatmeal and chips. Drop by tablespoons, about 3 inches apart, on the prepared baking sheet. Bake for 10 to 12 minutes, until golden. Cool on wire racks.

NOTE: These cookies may be stored for up to 3 days in an airtight container.

Cookies, Cookies, and More Cookies

I bake cookies for afternoon tea every day the inn is open. As you might imagine, I make a lot of cookies throughout the year! Since I'm committed to serving afternoon tea as part of the amenities we offer, I fulfill that promise by making it special each day. But I'll admit that occasionally I'm not in the mood for baking. Sometimes I'm working on something for dinner and find it difficult to change gears to bake cookies for tea. Sometimes I'm trying to watch my diet, and freshly baked cookies are tough to resist (let alone the cookie dough). Sometimes in summer, guests stay out a little later and aren't even back at the inn in time to enjoy them. By the end of December, I've baked so many renditions of holiday cookies that I can't bear to make another batch to give as gifts.

The redeeming thing is that our guests love the cookies. They knock on the kitchen door to tell me. They request the recipes and send me notes about how much their children enjoyed making them at home. They make it hard for me to "just say no" to baking cookies. Sometimes I do, though. I get downright radical in the kitchen. I bake brownies instead.

Walnut Brownies

These brownies are loved by our guests for their rich, fudgelike texture.

5 ounces bittersweet chocolate	½ cup packed light brown sugar
½ cup unsalted butter	1 teaspoon vanilla extract
1 large egg	½ cup all-purpose flour
½ teaspoon salt	½ cup chopped walnuts
½ cup granulated sugar	

1. Preheat the oven to 350°F. Butter an 8 × 8-inch baking pan, line it with parchment paper, and butter the parchment.

2. Melt the chocolate in a double boiler over simmering water. Stir in the butter until melted.

3. In a large bowl, whisk together the egg, salt, granulated sugar, brown sugar, and vanilla. Stir in the chocolate mixture. Add the flour and stir until just combined. Stir in the walnuts.

4. Spread the batter in the prepared pan, and bake for 30 to 40 minutes, until the top is shiny and the center is firm. Cool completely in the pan; remove from pan, peel off parchment, then slice into squares.

NOTE: These brownies may be made up to 48 hours in advance and stored in an airtight container.

Peanut Butter Cookies

Peanut butter cookies may be sandwiched with melted chocolate or grape jam for interesting variations.

½ cup unsalted butter, softened
½ cup packed light brown sugar
½ cup plus 2 tablespoons
    granulated sugar
1 large egg

¼ cup smooth peanut butter
1¼ cups all-purpose flour
½ teaspoon baking soda
½ teaspoon salt

---

1. Preheat the oven to 350°F. Lightly grease a baking sheet with solid shortening.

2. In a large bowl, beat the butter, brown sugar, and ½ cup granulated sugar with an electric mixer until fluffy. Beat in the egg and peanut butter. In another bowl, whisk together the flour, baking soda, and salt. Beat the dry mixture into the butter mixture until just combined. Form the dough into sixteen balls, each the size of a walnut. Place them on the prepared baking sheet, and bake for 5 minutes. Remove the sheet from the oven and press each cookie with the back of a fork, making indentations. Sprinkle the remaining 2 tablespoons granulated sugar over the cookies, and bake for 5 to 7 minutes longer, until flat and golden. Cool on wire racks.

NOTE: Press down carefully with the fork to avoid piercing the cookies or creating uneven lines.

The cookies may be stored for up to 3 days in an airtight container.

Butter Roll-Out Cookies

This is an all-purpose rolling dough that I use with a wide array of cookie cutters year-round. The cookies may be decorated with colored sugar before baking, dipped in confectioners' sugar while still warm, or iced after cooling.

---

1 cup unsalted butter, softened	½ teaspoon almond extract
1½ cups confectioners sugar	2½ cups all-purpose flour
1 large egg	1 teaspoon baking soda
1 tablespoon vanilla extract	1 teaspoon cream of tartar

---

1. In a large bowl, beat the butter and confectioners' sugar with an electric mixer until fluffy. Add the egg, vanilla, and almond extract and beat until combined. In another bowl, whisk together the flour, baking soda, and cream of tartar. Beat the flour mixture into the butter mixture until just combined. Divide the dough in half and form each half into a rectangle measuring approximately 4 × 5 inches. Wrap them individually in waxed paper, and refrigerate until firm, at least 1 hour or up to 24 hours.

2. Preheat the oven to 350°F.

3. Divide each block of dough in half and roll them out one half at a time, on a floured work surface. Cut the dough with cookie cutters, and use a spatula to transfer the cookies to a baking sheet. Bake for 10 to 12 minutes, until the edges are just beginning to brown. Transfer to wire racks and cool completely.

NOTE: If the dough has been refrigerated for longer than 2 hours, soften it by letting it stand at room temperature before rolling it out.

These cookies may be stored in airtight containers for up to 3 days.

DESSERTS

Everyone seems to be able to save room for a bite of dessert, but our guests have a hard time not finishing every last morsel of these favorites. Some are for chocolate lovers, while others take advantage of our home-grown berries and fruits. The seasonal recipes are perfect for holiday entertaining. I've included desserts here that even a novice will find easy to prepare.

Black and White Chocolate Crepe

SERVES 6

This dessert was part of a black and white formal dinner theme for our New Year's Eve celebration one year. Use a high-quality chocolate like Callebaut for the tastiest results. If you like to prepare desserts, it's economical and handy to buy the 10-pound blocks that pastry chefs use and store them in the freezer.

2¼ cups heavy cream

1 tablespoon powdered gelatin

8 ounces white chocolate, chopped

8 ounces bittersweet chocolate, chopped

¾ cup all-purpose flour

¼ cup Dutch-process cocoa powder

3 tablespoons sugar

1 large egg

1 large egg yolk

¾ cup half-and-half

---

1. Combine 1 cup of the heavy cream and the gelatin in a medium saucepan. Allow the gelatin to soften for 5 minutes. Then add the white chocolate and place the pan over low heat. Stir constantly until the chocolate is melted, about 3 minutes. Allow to cool, stirring occasionally to prevent the gelatin from setting. In a mixing bowl, beat 1 cup of the heavy cream until it forms soft peaks. Fold the whipped cream into the white chocolate mixture, and refrigerate until ready to serve.

2. Make the sauce: Melt the bittersweet chocolate in a double boiler over simmering water. Whisk in the remaining ¼ cup heavy cream until smooth. Refrigerate until serving time.

3. Whisk the flour, cocoa powder, and sugar together in a large mixing bowl. In a separate bowl, whisk together the egg, egg yolk, half-and-half, and ¼ cup water. Stir the egg mixture into the dry mixture until just combined.

4. Heat a 7- or 8-inch nonstick crepe pan (or use nonstick cooking spray in a regular skillet). Ladle about ¼ cup of the batter into the pan and swirl it quickly to cover the inside surface of the pan. Cook over medium heat until the crepe begins to brown at the edges and loosen, 1½ to 2 minutes. Flip the crepe over and cook for 20 seconds longer. Remove the crepe from the pan and allow to cool. Repeat until six crepes are completed.

5. Divide the white chocolate filling among the six crepes, and roll up each crepe. Warm the chocolate sauce slightly, and drizzle it over the crepes. Serve immediately.

NOTE: To break up large blocks of chocolate, double-bag the block in plastic bags, place it on a concrete or other hard surface, and bang it with a hammer until the chunks are the desired size.

The small amount of gelatin added to the white chocolate mousse adds body to the filling.

NOTES FROM THE INN:
THE NEW YEAR'S EVE EVENT

Each year since we opened, we have offered a two-night New Year's Eve package. Typically guests arrive on the thirtieth for a wine and hors d'oeuvre get-together. It's very informal, so guests get a chance to meet and become acquainted with each other. Bob and I act as hosts, so for us it's like having a wonderful house party. Some of the guests have been returning for years, but there are always some new people to get to know.

On New Year's Eve, we serve an elaborate multi-course dinner and then gather in front of the fireplace for a midnight champagne toast. For the millennium New Year's Eve, we poured everyone a glass of Dom Perignon, but typically the guests bring their own champagne. We play some good music and monitor the countdown on television with the volume muted. It's a relaxing, low-key way to enjoy the New Year—no forced kissing of strangers, no one getting out of control.

Although some people wear black tie, it's not required—everyone wears whatever feels comfortable. One year two young couples who were traveling together outdressed everyone by donning sequined gowns and silk tuxedos. They looked terrific, like something out of a luxury car commercial. Around 11:30 they must have gotten tired of being dressed up. They went upstairs, changed into pajamas, and came down in robes and fuzzy slippers for the champagne toast. No one even flinched! New Year's Eve is one opportunity when we really get to interact with guests and enjoy their company. It's a great way for us to toast another wonderful year at the inn. I may just wear *my* fuzzy slippers this year to celebrate.

White Chocolate Crème Brûlée

SERVES 6

Popular desserts such as crème brûlée often remain customer favorites long after they're considered "out" by food writers. I try to avoid being judgmental about food preferences and stick with giving my guests what they really want. This white chocolate version has always been one of our most requested desserts, and it's wonderfully easy to make. The white chocolate makes a creamy custard that's the perfect foil to the crisp sugar brûlée topping.

1½ cups heavy cream

1 cup whole milk

½ cup plus 1 tablespoon sugar

8 ounces white chocolate, chopped

6 large egg yolks

---

1. Preheat the oven to 350°F.

2. Combine the cream, milk, and ½ cup sugar in a medium-size saucepan and bring to a boil. Remove from the heat and stir in the white chocolate until melted. Allow to cool slightly.

3. Whisk the egg yolks into the white chocolate mixture. Divide the mixture among six individual ramekins or crème brûlée dishes. Place the ramekins in a roasting pan, and add enough boiling water to come halfway up the sides of the ramekins. Bake for 20 minutes, until set but not brown. Allow to cool, and then refrigerate for at least 2 hours.

4. When you are ready to serve the dessert, sprinkle each custard with a thin, even layer of the remaining 1 tablespoon sugar, about ½ teaspoon per ramekin. Using a hand-held propane torch (or by running under a preheated broiler), brown the top quickly and evenly—do not heat up the custard. Serve immediately.

NOTE: The custard may be made up to 48 hours ahead and refrigerated. Wait until just before serving to caramelize the top.

The Dessert Tray

In the early days of the restaurant, we found that showing the desserts on a tray was a sure way to get a reluctant customer to order one. We always had a few desserts that couldn't go on the tray, but we tried to keep everything that we showed looking fresh and irresistible. It must have worked, because once two women ordered the entire selection. On another occasion, an elderly customer plucked a piece of cake right off the tray. The waitress assured her we'd cut her a fresh piece, and bring a plate too.

I used to make at least five dessert choices for the tray, plus a selection of homemade sorbets or other frozen desserts. Now we offer a single dessert choice with several different components that are a variation on a theme, such as the "Belgian Chocolate Trio" or one I named "Just Peachy." This allows me to concentrate a little more on how I present the dessert, although the taste is still what guests remember most. Sometimes I'll even offer a sampling of several different desserts. But I know that some of our guests probably miss the dessert tray—especially those women who ordered all five.

Chocolate Chunk Bread Pudding

The bread is cut into chunks for this chocolatey pudding so that it retains some of its texture. Baking the bread puddings in a water bath creates a creamy custard.

1½ cups heavy cream
1½ cups whole milk
¼ cup sugar
12 ounces bittersweet chocolate,
    coarsely chopped
4 large eggs

4 large egg yolks
¼ cup unsalted butter, melted
Six 1-inch-thick slices Simple
    Brioche Loaf (page 62) or
    challah, cut into cubes

---

1. Preheat the oven to 325°F. Butter six ramekins.

2. Combine the cream, milk, and sugar in a medium-size saucepan and bring just to a boil. Remove from the heat and stir in 8 ounces of the chocolate until melted. Whisk in the eggs, egg yolks, and melted butter.

3. Place the brioche cubes in a large mixing bowl and pour the chocolate custard over them, stirring until all the liquid is absorbed. Then fold in the remaining bittersweet chocolate pieces. Divide the mixture among the prepared ramekins, and place them in a roasting pan. Add enough boiling water to come halfway up the sides of the ramekins, and bake for 20 minutes, until set. Serve warm.

VARIATION: Substitute 4 ounces coarsely chopped white chocolate for the 4 ounces bittersweet chocolate that is folded in at the end.

NOTE: White Chocolate Ice Cream (page 198) is the perfect accompaniment.

    The bread puddings may be made up to 24 hours in advance and refrigerated. Reheat them in a water bath in a 325°F oven for 8 minutes, or in the microwave on high power for 1 minute. They're also delicious at room temperature.

Simple Hot Fudge Sauce

MAKES 1¼ CUPS

Here's an easy way to dress up any chocolate dessert or to turn ordinary ice cream into a deluxe sundae. Use a squeeze bottle to drizzle a little sauce on a white dessert plate for an elegant presentation.

2 tablespoons corn syrup
⅔ cup heavy cream
8 ounces bittersweet chocolate, finely chopped

Bring the corn syrup and cream just to a boil in a small saucepan, and remove from heat. Stir in the chocolate until melted. Whisk until all the chocolate is incorporated. Refrigerate for up to 2 days if not using immediately.

Dessert for Three

We had a great team of waitress and dishwasher/busperson in two of our earliest staff members, Karen and Kevin. They made it easy for me to concentrate on my job as chef, instead of having to try to manage the dining room from the kitchen. We all shared a desire to do a good job. The other thing we all shared was a love of chocolate desserts. At the end of the evening, I would prepare an extra-large serving of whatever special chocolate dessert I had prepared that day—maybe the Black and White Chocolate Crepes or the Chocolate Waffles with White Chocolate Ice Cream. Kevin would get three forks and we'd all dive in. We didn't stop until we had finished the entire dessert. Karen would taste her first bite, turn her eyes skyward, and say, "I think I've died and gone to heaven." I still consider that to be the nicest compliment I've ever received about a dessert.

Chocolate Waffles with White Chocolate Ice Cream

SERVES 6

White chocolate makes the creamiest ice cream. You'll need an ice cream machine to make it at home, but it's worth the effort. I sometimes make the waffles in a heart-shaped iron for a special Valentine's Day dessert. For an especially decadent treat, top these with the Simple Hot Fudge Sauce on page 197.

1 quart half-and-half	4 teaspoons baking powder
14 large egg yolks	1 teaspoon salt
⅔ cup sugar	2 cups whole milk
10 ounces white chocolate, chopped	1 cup unsalted butter, melted
2 cups all-purpose flour	4 large egg whites
½ cup Dutch-process cocoa powder	Confectioners' sugar, for dusting

1. Bring the half-and-half just to a boil in a large saucepan. In a large bowl, whisk 10 egg yolks with the sugar. Whisk in the hot half-and-half, and pour the mixture back into the saucepan. Stir the mixture over low heat until it thickens slightly, 10 to 12 minutes. Remove the pan from the heat and stir in the white chocolate until melted. Place the mixture in a metal mixing bowl, set the bowl into a bowl of ice water, and whisk until cooled. Process according to the directions for your ice cream machine.

2. Preheat a square Belgian waffle iron. Combine the flour, cocoa powder, baking powder, and salt in a medium-size bowl. In another bowl, whisk together the remaining 4 egg yolks, the milk, and the melted butter. Stir this into the dry ingredients until just combined. In a separate bowl, whip the egg whites until they form soft peaks. Fold them into the batter. Ladle some of the batter into the waffle iron and bake according to the manufacturer's directions. Repeat until six sets of waffles are cooked. Fill the waffles with the white chocolate ice cream, dust with confectioners' sugar, and serve.

NOTE: The waffles may be made ahead and reheated. They also freeze well for up to 2 weeks.

Chocolate Soufflés

SERVES 6

This is a stable version of a soufflé that gives you time to get the dessert onto the plates without having it fall. Sweetened whipped cream is a delicious accompaniment.

---

12 ounces bittersweet chocolate
1 cup unsalted butter
6 large egg whites

¾ cup sugar
4 large egg yolks
⅔ cup all-purpose flour

---

1. Preheat the oven to 400°F. Butter six individual soufflé cups.

2. Melt the chocolate and butter in a double boiler over simmering water. Remove from the heat and allow to cool slightly.

3. In the meantime, beat the egg whites with an electric mixer until they form soft peaks. Still beating, gradually add the sugar until it is combined and the peaks are stiff.

4. Whisk the egg yolks into the chocolate mixture until smooth. Whisk in the flour. Then fold in the whipped egg whites. Divide the mixture among the prepared soufflé cups. Place the cups on a baking sheet, and bake for 15 to 20 minutes, until the edges are set. Serve immediately.

NOTE: The batter may be refrigerated for up to 24 hours. Allow extra time to bring it to room temperature before baking.

Chocolate Mocha Pie

This creamy pie with a candy bar crust must be made at least 3 hours ahead to give it time to set up in the refrigerator.

---

1 cup all-purpose flour

1⅓ cups packed light brown sugar

1⅓ cups cold unsalted butter

3 tablespoons chopped semisweet
    chocolate

¾ cup finely chopped pecans

5 teaspoons instant coffee granules

3 ounces bittersweet chocolate,
    melted

4 large eggs

2 cups heavy cream

½ cup confectioners' sugar

2 tablespoons Dutch-process cocoa
    powder

⅓ cup bittersweet chocolate
    shavings

---

1. Preheat the oven to 350°F.

2. Combine the flour and ⅓ cup of the brown sugar in a food processor (or use a pastry blender). Add ⅓ cup of the butter in bits, and process until crumbly. Add the chocolate, pecans, and 2 tablespoons cold water, and pulse briefly until the dough sticks together. Press the mixture evenly into the bottom and sides of a 9-inch pie pan. Bake for 15 to 18 minutes, until just golden. Allow to cool completely before filling.

3. Combine the remaining 1 cup butter, the coffee granules, melted chocolate, and remaining 1 cup brown sugar in a large bowl, and beat with an electric mixer until smooth. Add the eggs one at a time, beating until smooth after each addition. Spoon the mixture into the pie shell, smoothing the top. Refrigerate for at least 3 hours, until the filling is firm and thoroughly chilled.

4. Just before serving, whip the cream, confectioners' sugar, and cocoa powder together until stiff. Spread on top of the chilled pie, or use a pastry bag to pipe on rosettes. Garnish with the chocolate shavings, and serve.

NOTE: This pie is also delicious frozen. Dip the knife in hot water before slicing a frozen version.

Fudge Pecan Tart

SERVES 8

Pecan pie purists beware: One taste of this version with bittersweet chocolate chunks will convince you that some classics can be improved upon. Allow the tart to cool completely before serving.

1¾ cups all-purpose flour

¼ cup solid vegetable shortening

½ cup cold unsalted butter

¾ cup packed light brown sugar

3 large eggs

2 teaspoons vanilla extract

1 cup light corn syrup

1½ cups pecan halves

5 ounces bittersweet chocolate, coarsely chopped

---

1. Preheat the oven to 400°F.

2. Combine 1½ cups of the flour, the shortening, and ¼ cup of the butter in a food processor, and process until crumbly. Sprinkle in 2 tablespoons cold water, and process until the dough begins to form a ball (add a little more water if necessary). Press the dough evenly into a 10-inch tart pan with a removable bottom, and prick it all over with a fork. Bake the shell for 12 to 15 minutes, until just beginning to brown. Let it cool completely. Leave the oven on.

3. In a mixing bowl, combine the remaining ¼ cup flour with the brown sugar, eggs, vanilla, and corn syrup. Beat with an electric mixer until blended. Melt the remaining ¼ cup butter and stir into the mixture. Stir in the pecans and the chocolate chunks. Pour the batter into the cooled shell and bake for 10 minutes. Reduce the temperature to 350°F and bake for 30 to 40 minutes, until the edges are puffed and the center is just set (it will firm up as it cools). Allow the tart to cool completely before removing the sides of the tart pan.

NOTES FROM THE INN:
THE WEB SITE

When it comes to technological advances at the inn, I will freely admit that I drag my feet. In this area, I believe in the adage "If it isn't broken, don't fix it," so when Bob started pestering me about doing a Web site, I was skeptical. We had just recently designed and printed beautiful color brochures. Our occupancy rates were consistently good. So why bother?

I actually had never been on the Internet and was a little suspicious of it. How could we project the warm qualities of our inn in the remoteness of cyberspace? Part of Bob's enthusiasm stemmed from the fact that he had a couple of students who were computer experts and would implement the site for us. All I had to do was design the content. For someone who had never seen a Web site before, this was daunting. So I started by doing a little research. I selected some inns that we had enjoyed staying at over the years and checked out their sites. I looked at some award-winning product sites that I'd read about in business magazines. I realized that just as in print advertising, the sites I liked best delivered the most information in the most visually pleasing layout. I also found that any site that took too long to download was a site I might never see.

Our Web site is a simple and direct source of information about the inn, with a lot of beautiful photographs. The home page lists all the essentials—the number of rooms, the price range, and the amenities we offer—and then invites the visitor to go to specific topic areas. It has the look of a beautiful color brochure but it is much more extensive than anything we could afford to print and mail out. There are no bells and whistles, nothing that takes forever to download, and no personal letters from the innkeepers. It represents us and our inn well. It is also one of the best and most cost-effective advertising pieces we have.

It took Bob a few months to convince me to do it, and a little time for me to learn to communicate with the computer guys. They were invaluable in steering me through the computer aspect of the Web design, and now I feel that I know a lot about the technology aspects of the Web. We're now members of the cyber community with our own dot-com address. It's really exciting to be on the cutting edge of technology. Just don't try to e-mail me. I still prefer the phone.

Raspberry and White Chocolate Tarts

SERVES 6

This is the closest thing we have ever had to a "signature" dessert, since I've offered it every year for Valentine's Day. I use heart-shaped tart pans with removable bottoms to make my Valentine's version, but you can use round pans instead. In the days when we had a dessert tray to show off their enticing appearance, every couple ordered at least one of these heart-shaped tarts.

1½ cups all-purpose flour

½ cup plus 2 tablespoons sugar

6 tablespoons cold unsalted butter, cut into ¼-inch pieces

2 tablespoons solid vegetable shortening

16 ounces white chocolate, chopped

1 cup plus 2 tablespoons heavy cream

4 large egg whites

12 ounces frozen raspberries, thawed

2 pints fresh raspberries

⅓ cup seedless raspberry jam

18 large white chocolate shavings

---

1. Combine the flour, 2 tablespoons sugar, the butter, and shortening in a food processor, and process until crumbly. Add cold water 1 tablespoon at a time until the dough sticks together. Wrap the dough in plastic wrap and refrigerate for 30 minutes.

2. In the meantime, preheat the oven to 350°F.

3. Lightly butter six individual tart pans with removable bottoms. Divide the dough into six balls, and on a lightly floured surface roll out each to fit into the tart pans, trimming off any excess. Prick the dough all over, place the pans on a baking sheet, and bake for 15 to 20 minutes, until golden. Cool completely in the pans. Remove the tarts from the pans and set on a rack.

4. Combine 4 ounces of the white chocolate with the 2 tablespoons heavy cream in a double boiler, and heat over simmering water, stirring constantly, until the chocolate is melted and smooth. Spread the melted chocolate in the bottom of the tart shells and allow to cool.

5. Bring the remaining 1 cup cream just to a boil in a saucepan, and remove from the heat. Add the remaining 12 ounces white chocolate, and stir until melted. Allow to cool but not harden.

6. In the meantime, beat the egg whites and ¼ cup of the sugar with an electric mixer until glossy. Place over simmering water and whisk until the egg whites are hot. Remove from the heat and whip until cool. Fold the meringue into the white chocolate mixture, and divide it among the six tarts.

7. Combine the frozen raspberries with the remaining ¼ cup sugar in a food processor or blender, and process until smooth. Strain, discarding the seeds, and set aside.

8. Toss the fresh raspberries with the jam, and arrange them on top of the six tarts. Spoon the raspberry sauce around the tarts, and garnish with the chocolate shavings. Serve immediately.

NOTE: The tart shells may be made up to 24 hours in advance and stored in an airtight container. The raspberry sauce may be made up to 24 hours in advance and stored in the refrigerator. Spoon the filling into the tart shells and arrange the raspberries just before serving.

Raspberries All Summer Long

I had always assumed that raspberries had a short growing season, since they appear at our local farm stands just briefly in early summer. Since I've started growing my own, I've found that the key to a sustained harvest is to plant a variety of types.

Our first to bear fruit are Taylor, which produce large, well-formed berries that melt in your mouth (it's a wonder any make it to the inn's breakfast table some mornings!). They begin to ripen in early July and remain productive for 3 or 4 weeks.

We also grow Heritage Red, which produces fruit throughout August and September. Our gold varieties, Tulameen, Kiwi, and Fall Gold, begin producing in July and continue right until the first frost. So we have a continuous harvest, from early July right until the end of October.

If you're thinking of planting raspberries, keep in mind that they grow and spread rapidly and can be fairly invasive. Ours require constant pruning to keep them from overtaking other parts of the garden. I've also started planting another stalwart plant, the sunflower, on the border of the raspberry beds to help keep them in check. The sight of the various brown and gold sunflowers peeking out over the picket fence, along with the plump raspberries overflowing our picking baskets, is a sure sign of summer at the inn.

Strawberry Stuffed French Toast

This dessert rendition of one of our guests' breakfast favorites is best made when strawberries are at the peak of their growing season. Use a fluted round cookie cutter to give the brioche slices a decorative shape.

8 ounces mascarpone, softened	Twelve ½-inch-thick slices Simple
5 tablespoons sugar	Brioche Loaf (page 62) or challah
¾ cup heavy cream	4 tablespoons unsalted butter
2 pints fresh strawberries, hulled	2 tablespoons corn oil
and sliced lengthwise	¼ cup Grand Marnier
3 large eggs	Confectioners' sugar, for dusting

1. Combine the mascarpone and 2 tablespoons of the sugar in a bowl, and beat with an electric mixer until smooth. In another bowl, whip ½ cup of the cream until it forms soft peaks. Fold the whipped cream into the mascarpone. Fold in half of the strawberries, and set aside.

2. In a shallow bowl, whisk together the eggs and the remaining ¼ cup cream. Dip each slice of bread into the egg mixture, coating each side evenly. Heat 2 tablespoons of the butter and the corn oil in a large skillet until the butter is melted and foamy. Sauté the brioche until golden on both sides, 1 to 2 minutes per side. Allow to cool about 5 minutes.

3. Place six pieces of French toast on individual plates. Spread the mascarpone mixture over them. Press the remaining six pieces on top to form a sandwich.

4. Melt the remaining 2 tablespoons butter in a medium-size saucepan. Add the remaining strawberries, and sprinkle with the remaining 3 tablespoons sugar. Add the Grand Marnier, flame if desired (remove the pan from the heat, and standing as far back as possible, ignite the liquid with a long match; swirl the pan around until the flame dies out), and cook for 1 minute. Spoon the sauce onto the French toast, dust with confectioners' sugar, and serve.

So Many Strawberries, So Little Time

We grow our own tiny alpine strawberries, but we also look forward to the availability of the larger varieties grown by local farmers. There's an abundance of strawberries for sale at all of the local farm stands each June. Different varieties yield different sizes and varying degrees of sweetness. The weather is also often a factor. Never buy strawberries that were picked just after a rain; they absorb the water very easily. To clean the berries, fill a bowl with fresh water, swirl them around in it to loosen any dirt, and immediately remove them to drain in a colander.

My favorite grower is located just minutes from the inn. Each morning in strawberry season, I drive down to pick up a few fresh quarts before breakfast. Their large, sweet berries are a beautiful deep red all the way through. They also sell them in the woven baskets they use to pick them. These baskets make them completely irresistible. I love to bring home a basket, drop a few of the biggest ones into cold water, and test them out for my guests.

Cinnamon Peach Pie

SERVES 8 TO 10

Once the local peach harvest begins, I find ways to use peaches in every meal we serve. This easy-to-assemble cinnamon peach pie allows the flavor and sweetness of the peaches to shine through.

---

2 cups all-purpose flour
1 teaspoon salt
15 tablespoons cold unsalted butter
3 tablespoons solid vegetable
    shortening

1¼ cups sugar
1 tablespoon ground cinnamon
6 peaches, peeled, pitted, and
    sliced
1 teaspoon fresh lemon juice

---

1. Preheat the oven to 425°F.

2. Combine the flour and salt in a large bowl. Using a pastry blender, cut in 12 tablespoons of the butter and all the vegetable shortening until the mixture is crumbly. Add cold water, a tablespoon at a time, until the mixture sticks together. Divide the pastry in half, and roll each piece into a ball. Roll out each ball on a lightly floured surface to form a 12-inch round. Press one crust into a 10-inch deep-dish pie pan and prick the bottom with a fork.

3. Combine the sugar and cinnamon in a medium-size bowl. Sprinkle the peaches with lemon juice and toss them with the sugar mixture. Pour the peaches into the pan and dot the top with the remaining 3 table-spoons butter. Fold the remaining crust in half and place it on top of the filling. Unfold it and press the outer edges together. Cut vents into the center with a sharp knife, and cover the edge with a strip of aluminum foil to prevent excessive browning. Place on a baking sheet and bake for 25 minutes. Remove the foil and bake for 10 to 15 minutes longer, until the juice begins to bubble through the vents. Allow to cool slightly before serving.

VARIATION: Substitute 4 cups fresh blueberries for the peaches.

In Praise of the Humble Pie

Whatever happened to pie baking? Sometimes I think it's becoming a lost art. It's rare to find a pie for sale at a bakery, even more rare to find a tasty one. Perhaps it's considered too plain for bakery fare. But the plainness of the pie is actually what makes it a standout dessert.

Pies are a great way of accenting nature's best work. Think of the perfection of ripe, juicy peaches or fresh wild blueberries. Why work hard at preparing a complex dessert when really all you need to do is to showcase the flawlessness of the fruit itself? This is where the humble pie is at its best. Pies allow nature's perfection to shine through. The bonus is that they're so easy to make. Add a flaky crust or perhaps a streusel topping, and you're ready to go.

So when your favorite fruit is at its seasonal best, bake a pie. You'll be amazed, as I often am, how something so simple can create so much enjoyment for your guests.

Pumpkin Mousse and Gingersnap Parfait

SERVES 6

Pumpkin mousse is another all-time favorite dessert at the inn, especially when layered with our homemade gingersnaps. The cookies may be made up to 2 days ahead, but beware—they're so tasty they may not last.

6 tablespoons unsalted butter, softened	2 teaspoons ground ginger
1½ cups sugar	2 teaspoons ground cinnamon
1 large egg	2 teaspoons powdered gelatin
3 tablespoons molasses	½ cup brandy
1⅓ cups all-purpose flour	2 cups canned pumpkin puree
1 teaspoon baking soda	½ teaspoon ground nutmeg
½ teaspoon salt	¼ teaspoon ground cloves
	2 cups heavy cream

1. Preheat the oven to 350°F. Lightly grease a baking sheet with solid shortening.

2. In a large bowl, blend the butter and ½ cup of the sugar with an electric mixer. Add the egg and molasses and blend until smooth. In a small bowl, combine the flour, baking soda, salt, 1 teaspoon of the ginger, and 1 teaspoon of the cinnamon. Add the dry mixture all at once to the dough, and blend. Roll a tablespoon of dough into a ball, and place it on the prepared baking sheet. Continue until all the dough is shaped, placing the balls about 3 inches apart. Bake for 15 to 18 minutes, until the cookies have spread and crackled. Cool completely on wire racks.

3. In the meantime, sprinkle the gelatin over the brandy in a small ramekin. Set the ramekin in a small skillet filled with simmering water, and stir until the gelatin is dissolved.

4. Combine the pumpkin, remaining 1 cup sugar, remaining 1 teaspoon ginger, remaining 1 teaspoon cinnamon, the nutmeg, and the cloves in a large bowl. Whisk in the warm gelatin mixture. Whip the cream to soft peaks in another bowl, and fold it into the pumpkin.

5. Reserve six of the cookies. Process the remaining cookies in a food processor until crumbly. Spoon a few tablespoons of the pumpkin mousse into each of six parfait or other deep stemmed glasses. Sprinkle with cookie crumbs and add another layer of mousse. Continue alternating layers, ending with mousse as the top layer. Cover and refrigerate until set, at least 15 minutes. Garnish each parfait with a gingersnap, and serve.

NOTE: The parfaits may be assembled up to 2 hours before serving.

Taming the Great Pumpkin

I always found the idea of using real pumpkin intimidating. So when I had the opportunity to choose the topic for an autumn cooking demonstration, I decided to seize the moment and work out my "issues" with pumpkins. When I asked around at the local farm stands which types tasted best, I got a wide range of answers. So I chose smaller pumpkins of several different varieties (easier to carry) and tried using them in new ways. I peeled and grated (Pumpkin, Wild Rice, and Apricots on page 153), I roasted and scooped (Pumpkin Bread Pudding on page 212), and I sautéed and pureed (Pumpkin Soup on page 99). I didn't notice an appreciable difference in the various types, except that the color of the flesh varied from pale yellow to a deeper orange. Smaller pumpkins seemed easier to handle and yielded more flesh per pound.

The demo was a great success. If you'd like to expand your horizons and use fresh pumpkin puree for the Pumpkin Bread Pudding, here's how to prepare it: Preheat the oven to 350°F. Cut the pumpkin in half, remove the stem, and scoop out the seeds. Place the pumpkin, cut side down, in a roasting pan and add 1 inch of water. Cover with aluminum foil and bake until tender, about 1 hour. Remove from the pan and allow to cool completely. Scoop out the flesh and discard the skin. Puree the flesh in a food processor or blender until smooth. This makes about 4 cups of puree.

Pumpkin Bread Pudding
with Caramel Sauce

SERVES 6

Even guests who claim they don't like pumpkin have enjoyed this custardy bread pudding and its enticing caramel sauce.

---

2 cups heavy cream
1 cup half-and-half
½ cup packed light brown sugar
1¼ cups granulated sugar
3 large eggs
3 large egg yolks
2 cups pumpkin puree, fresh
(see page 211)

1 teaspoon ground cinnamon
½ teaspoon ground nutmeg
½ teaspoon ground ginger
½ teaspoon ground allspice
Five 1-inch-thick slices Simple
Brioche Loaf (page 62) or
challah, cut into cubes

---

1. Preheat the oven to 350°F. Butter six small ramekins.

2. Combine 1 cup heavy cream with the half-and-half in a medium saucepan, and bring to a boil. Stir in the brown sugar and ¼ cup granulated sugar, and remove from the heat. In a medium bowl, whisk the eggs, egg yolks, pumpkin puree, and spices until combined. Whisk the hot cream into the pumpkin mixture until combined.

3. Place the brioche cubes in a large mixing bowl and pour the pumpkin mixture over them, stirring until all the liquid is absorbed. Divide the mixture among the ramekins and place them in a roasting pan. Add enough boiling water to come halfway up the sides of the ramekins, and bake for 20 minutes, until set.

4. In the meantime, combine the remaining 1 cup granulated sugar with ⅓ cup water in a medium saucepan. Without stirring, cook over low heat until dark amber in color, about 20 minutes. Remove from the heat and submerge the bottom of the pan in a bowl of cold water to stop the cooking. Add the remaining 1 cup heavy cream and return the pan to low heat, stirring constantly until the caramel melts and the cream is incorporated, about 10 minutes. To serve, transfer the bread puddings from the ramekins to dessert plates, and spoon on the warm caramel sauce.

NOTE: Use caution when making the caramel, since any skin contact can cause a severe burn. Stop cooking the caramel just before you think it's done—it will continue to darken even after the pan is submerged in cold water. If the caramel turns too dark, discard it and start over. I use a stainless-steel-lined saucepan, since you can see the color more clearly than in anodized aluminum. Burnt caramel smells terrible, so pay close attention to the caramel once it starts to turn color. Clean the pan of any residue by boiling water in it.

The Orchard

We call our small collection of fruit trees "the orchard" even though they take up little space on our grounds. The idea for the orchard actually was conceived at a nursery auction—Bob just couldn't pass up those $5 fruit trees. Three of the trees are dwarf Liberty apples. The fourth lost its tag on the way home from the auction and is referred to as the "Mystery" apple. Its fruit is larger than the Liberty's, but it is delicious.

The first year I ignored the orchard, wondering whether the trees would actually survive. They did, and I quickly learned that fruit trees require some diligence to protect them from pests, diseases, and tall critters that will take a bite out of each and every piece of fruit. I've taken over tending the orchard, heartlessly thinning the tiny fruits in spring and monitoring the developing fruits all summer for signs of attack. I've also added some dwarf white peach trees, although so far these seem even more prone to attack than the apples and have yielded only a few peaches.

This year we harvested several bushels of apples on a crisp October day. We felt rather happy about the orchard, marveling at how such a small investment, treated with a heavy dose of tender loving care, could yield so much joy. As always, our guests were part of this joy, able to share in the bounty of the orchard through an array of fresh apple dishes.

Apple Sour Cream Pie

Our tiny apple trees yield enough fruit to make several of these creamy apple pies.

1½ cups all-purpose flour
½ teaspoon salt
14 tablespoons unsalted butter
1½ tablespoons solid vegetable shortening, chilled
1 cup granulated sugar
3 large eggs

1½ cups sour cream
2 teaspoons ground cinnamon
1 teaspoon vanilla extract
5 apples, such as McIntosh or Rome, peeled, cored, and thinly sliced
¼ cup packed light brown sugar

---

1. Preheat the oven to 350°F.

2. Combine 1 cup of the flour and the salt in a food processor (or use a pastry blender). Add 6 tablespoons of the butter and all the vegetable shortening, and pulse until the mixture is crumbly. Add cold water, 1 tablespoon at a time, pulsing until the mixture sticks together. Roll the pastry into a ball, and then roll it out on a lightly floured surface to form a 12-inch round. Press the crust into a 10-inch deep-dish pie pan, and prick the bottom with a fork.

3. In a large bowl, blend together ¾ cup of the granulated sugar, ¼ cup of the flour, and the eggs. Stir in the sour cream, 1 teaspoon of the cinnamon, and the vanilla. Toss the apple slices with the sour cream mixture, and spoon them into the pie crust. Place the pie on a baking sheet, and bake for 20 minutes.

4. In the meantime, combine the remaining ¼ cup granulated sugar, the brown sugar, the remaining ¼ cup flour, and the remaining 1 teaspoon cinnamon in a small bowl. Using a pastry blender, cut in the remaining 8 tablespoons butter until crumbly. Sprinkle the topping over the pie, and bake for another 25 to 30 minutes, until the topping is browned. Cool completely before serving.

The Girl

Although I introduce myself by name to arriving guests, some of them don't realize that I'm one of the owners of the inn. They also often don't realize that I'm the chef. This is an awkward and sometimes funny situation, because people make some erroneous assumptions. For example, they might be curious to know what's on the dinner menu, so they'll ask me if I know what "he," i.e., the chef, is making that night. I'll then explain that I'm the chef and end the confusion. They might also ask things about me in the third person, like "How long have the owners run the inn?" I can easily reply, "We opened in 1990," and subtly let them know who I am.

However, sometimes guests make it difficult to correct their mistaken assumptions. Older guests have on occasion referred to me as "the girl." Usually these comments are addressed to Bob. They range from true statements like "The girl told me it's okay to leave my car there," to requests like "Is the girl available to get us some ice?" to downright fabrications like "We spoke to the girl and she was supposed to change our dinner reservation" or "The girl never told us to bring our own wine." At some point, they usually find out who "the girl" really is, because we tell them in some tactful, nonthreatening way. They might ask Bob, "When will we meet your wife?" and he'll answer with a smile, "What do you mean? You already have!"

I'm always amazed that people assume that an innkeeper must be a certain age. It must be because many people believe that running an inn is something you do when you retire from your "real" job. Some people do retire to innkeeping, but not to the service-intensive type of inn that we run. If you plan to run an inn like ours as a retirement business, you need to realize that you won't really be retiring at all. You'll basically be going from one job to a different job, albeit perhaps a more enjoyable one.

So when people refer to me as "the girl," I don't take it personally. I know some people assume that I'm too young to own an inn. In some ways, it's a compliment. Thankfully, I'm actually old enough to appreciate being called "the girl." It's when someone calls me "Ma'am" that it really hurts!

Orange Champagne Granita

Granitas are easy-to-make alternatives to sorbets, and they're especially useful if you don't own an ice cream machine. The key to a good texture is to be consistent in scraping the crystals with a fork. Allowing the granita to set up too long between scrapings will make it chunky and granular instead of smooth. Try adding a scoop to a fruit soup for a refreshing dessert, or use it to enhance fresh fruit for an elegant brunch dish.

½ cup sugar

1½ cups orange juice

1½ cups dry champagne (or substitute club soda)

1. Place a 9 × 13-inch metal baking dish in the freezer to chill for at least 30 minutes.

2. Combine the sugar and 1 cup water in a small saucepan. Bring to a boil and cook over high heat until the sugar dissolves, about 5 minutes. Allow to cool completely.

3. Combine the orange juice and champagne in a large bowl. Stir the sugar syrup into the orange mixture, and pour the mixture into the chilled pan. Place the pan in the freezer and chill until ice crystals form around the edges, about 30 minutes. Remove the pan from the freezer and stir the mixture with a fork to incorporate the ice crystals. Continue freezing and stirring every 30 minutes until all the liquid is frozen, about 2 hours.

NOTE: Granitas may be made up to 48 hours in advance.

Frozen Lemon Mascarpone Mousse

Mascarpone, the Italian cheese that is used in creamy desserts like tiramisù, also yields lush results in this frozen mousse.

---

2 teaspoons powdered gelatin	3 large egg whites
½ cup fresh lemon juice	1 cup heavy cream
¾ cup sugar	4 ounces mascarpone

---

1. Sprinkle the gelatin over ¼ cup of the lemon juice in a small ramekin, and allow it to soften.

2. In the meantime, combine the sugar and egg whites in a double boiler and place it over simmering water. Whisk until the egg whites are hot and the sugar is dissolved, about 5 minutes. Remove from the heat and whip with an electric mixer until cooled and fluffy, about 5 minutes.

3. Set the ramekin in a pan of simmering water and stir until the gelatin dissolves. Pour the remaining ¼ cup lemon juice into a medium bowl and whisk in the warm gelatin. Fold in the egg whites. Whip the cream to soft peaks in another bowl, and fold into the lemon mixture. Fold in the mascarpone, and divide the mousse among six individual ramekins. Cover and freeze until firm, at least 2 hours.

NOTE: I like to spread this mousse into a 9 × 13-inch baking pan, freeze it, and then slice it into triangles for a unique presentation, or to use as a creamy frozen accent to another lemon dessert.

Lemon Sabayon with Raspberries

Lemon sabayon is a perfect refreshing finish to any meal but is particularly good after a rich entree. Guests looking for a little something lemony to end their dinner will enjoy the sweet and tart combination of this dessert.

---

12 ounces frozen red raspberries, thawed

1 cup sugar

4 large eggs

4 large egg yolks

1 cup fresh lemon juice

½ cup unsalted butter

½ cup heavy cream

1 pint fresh red raspberries

---

1. Combine the defrosted raspberries and ¼ cup of the sugar in a food processor or blender, and process until smooth. Press through a sieve to remove the seeds, and reserve the puree.

2. In a double boiler set over simmering water, whisk together the eggs, egg yolks, remaining ¾ cup sugar, and lemon juice. Continue cooking and whisking until frothy and thick, 6 to 8 minutes. Remove from the heat and whisk in the butter in bits. Set the pan in a bowl of ice water and continue whisking occasionally until cooled.

3. Whip the cream in a mixing bowl until it forms soft peaks, and fold into the lemon mixture. Divide the lemon mixture among six martini or other stemmed glasses, and swirl in the raspberry puree. Cover and refrigerate for at least 2 hours. Top with the fresh raspberries, and serve.

NOTE: The raspberry puree may be made up to 48 hours in advance. Add the fresh raspberries just before serving.

Pear and Cherry Clafouti

One of the neatest kitchen gadgets I've ever purchased is a cherry pitter. I don't use it often, but when I need to pit fresh cherries, it's invaluable. We have a huge gnarly cherry tree on our grounds that yields an abundance of golden fruits with just the slightest red tinge. Because the tree had never been pruned by the prior owners, the birds get to enjoy many of the cherries in its upper reaches. We're able to pick a few basketfuls from the lower branches to use in this custardy delight.

½ cup plus 1 tablespoon sugar

¾ cup half-and-half

¼ cup heavy cream

3 large eggs

1 teaspoon almond extract

½ cup almonds, finely ground

2 tablespoons butter, melted

⅔ cup all-purpose flour

1 pear, peeled, cored, and thinly sliced

1½ cups fresh cherries, pitted

Confectioners' sugar, for dusting

---

1. Preheat the oven to 350°F. Butter a 9- or 10-inch glass pie dish or fluted quiche pan, and dust the bottom with the 1 tablespoon sugar.

2. Combine the half-and-half, heavy cream, eggs, remaining ½ cup sugar, almond extract, almonds, melted butter, and flour in a food processor or blender, and process until smooth. Pour the batter into the prepared pan. Arrange the pear slices in a pinwheel pattern, pressing them into the batter. Fill the rest of the tart with the cherries, pressing them into the batter. Bake for 35 to 40 minutes, until the top is slightly puffed and golden brown and the batter is set. Dust with confectioners' sugar, slice into wedges, and serve.

NOTES FROM THE INN: PETS

We've always had pets at the inn, although as a guest you might never know it. We regard our pets as part of our family, and so they reside exclusively in our quarters. We do not allow guests to bring pets. We know that some of our guests would find it offensive to see animals, no matter how well behaved, being brought into the inn. Plus, many people have allergies to pet dander, which makes it impossible for most breeds of cats and dogs to stay in the inn without causing a problem for another guest. So our policy has always been to "just say no" to outside pets.

But our own pets are an important part of our lives. Our oldest pet is our cat, Peanut. He has a beautiful solid black coat that permanently bans him from the inn, since so many people are allergic to cat hair. He patrols our gardens each day and will occasionally allow our guests the rare pleasure (as he sees it) of petting him. He sleeps inside at night. When he's ready to be let out in the morning, Peanut has learned that a sure way of getting our immediate attention is to serenade us at the basement door when guests are having breakfast.

Our other pets have been miniature schnauzers. This breed sometimes has a reputation for being a little "yippy," but ours have always been quiet little dogs. (I know, I sound like some people talking about their children: "*Ours* are little angels!") Often when our guests see us walking them out in the yard, they'll comment that they never knew we had a dog. We take this as a supreme compliment. But when someone knocks at our residence door, they are loyal little terriers in defending our home. They're also great companions for me, lying by my desk while I do paperwork in the office or hanging around outside while I'm gardening.

Our first dog, Smokey, was my official food taster in the early days of the restaurant. (Don't yell at me, dog lovers; I now know how bad a lot of these foods are for dogs.) I used to call him "the gourmet dog." He is the only dog I know who would wiggle his tail if you mentioned osso buco or tiramisù. He used to get a little treat at the end of each restaurant night, courtesy of the dishwashers. Once while we were serving dinner, Smokey just couldn't wait until evening was over. He escaped into the inn and ran through the dining room, past our dumbfounded dinner guests, and announced his desire for his snack with a bark at the kitchen door.

Most of the time, though, our guests will see our dogs only when we're walking them. I know of one famous inn where the owners' regal Dalmatians are in the lobby to greet the guests before dinner (our state restaurant inspector would not be too keen on that idea). I've even heard of an inn in Key West where the innkeeper's Jack Russell terrier shows you to your room. But since we don't allow pets at the inn, I don't subject our guests to my pets, or in some cases, vice versa. I will admit that after some of our more challenging guests, we've thought about turning the inn into an exclusive pet hotel. There would certainly be less laundry to do. If the Inn at Twin Linden does become a deluxe pet resort, I'm sure we'll still have a gourmet menu in Smokey's honor.

Decking the Halls

I love decorating for the winter holidays, and I used to spend a lot of time making my own fresh decorations for the inn. I would take baskets into the gardens and cut boxwood and evergreens for my hand-fashioned wreaths. One year I even made all my own boxwood garlands (Bob has since nixed this creative urge, because he was sure I had overpruned the hedges!). When the large tree in the common area didn't seem festive enough for our participation in a holiday tour, I added smaller trees in the lobby and dining rooms. Early December became a holiday decorating marathon. It also became a little overwhelming.

In recent years, I've had to become much more efficient in my holiday plans. One reason is that the holidays follow right on the heels of our busiest season, autumn. It sometimes seems as if the fall is a three-month blur—we hit the ground running on Labor Day weekend and the next time we look up, it's Thanksgiving.

Another reason is the rush of the holidays by retailers. Their early decor creates the expectation that any public place will be fully decorated weeks before the holiday itself. One year, I received comments about how disappointed a guest had been that my tree wasn't up and decorated on the day after Thanksgiving. Now I begin decorating the inn in mid-November, just to make sure I have everything up by Thanksgiving weekend.

I refuse to be totally efficient and still insist on a freshly cut tree: I just haven't been able to give it up for a more sensible, but perhaps less sensual, artificial one. The cut tree makes the time critical. The tree is up so long that if it's not absolutely fresh and kept that way, it's a problem by New Year's Eve. It may begin as a beautifully shaped and fragrant display of sparkling lights, gold ribbon, and one-of-a-kind ornaments, but it can end up dried out if we're not diligent. We've tried all manner of preservatives and sprays, but we've realized it may just be impossible to keep a cut tree fresh for six or seven weeks.

We never sacrifice our personal enjoyment of the holidays to the business side of the inn—we close on major holidays so we can still spend them with our family. It may not make business sense, but it makes good personal sense to us. We even decorate our own freshly cut tree in our living quarters. So when you visit our inn, you'll find our festive holiday decor and a freshly cut tree to enjoy. However, you won't find us working on Christmas Day. And if you come by on New Year's Day, you'll find us closed for the one holiday when we'll actually be working: We've got to get that tree out of the inn before it sheds every last needle!

Eggnog Mousse

If you like eggnog, you'll love this light, airy mousse. It's one of our guests' favorites at holiday time.

---

2 cups half-and-half
1 vanilla bean, split
7 large egg yolks
⅔ cup sugar
1 teaspoon ground nutmeg

⅓ cup light corn syrup
5 large egg whites
½ cup heavy cream
Freshly grated nutmeg, for garnish

---

1. Combine the half-and-half and the vanilla bean in a medium saucepan, and bring to a boil. Remove the pan from the heat and set aside for the bean to soften, about 5 minutes. Scrape the vanilla bean seeds into the half-and-half and discard the pod. Whisk in the egg yolks and ⅓ cup of the sugar. Cook over low heat until the mixture is slightly thickened, about 5 minutes. Pour the mixture into a metal bowl, set it in a bowl of ice water, and whisk until cooled. Stir in the ground nutmeg and refrigerate.

2. Combine the remaining ⅓ cup sugar with the corn syrup and ⅓ cup water in a medium saucepan. Bring to a boil and cook until the mixture reaches the soft ball stage (240°F on a candy thermometer), about 5 minutes.

3. Whisk the egg whites with an electric mixer until they form soft peaks. With the mixer running, pour the sugar mixture down the side of the bowl and continue beating until the whites are cool and doubled in volume, 5 to 7 minutes. In another bowl, whip the cream until it forms soft peaks.

4. Fold the egg whites into the cooled custard; then fold in the whipped cream. Divide the mixture among six martini glasses or custard cups, and refrigerate until thoroughly chilled, about 1 hour. Garnish with freshly grated nutmeg just before serving.

INDEX

and smoked salmon soufflés, 16–17
Gorgonzola:
  -sausage frittata, 30
  -shallot vinaigrette, spinach with
    pancetta and, 106
  and wilted spinach omelet roll, 43
granita, orange champagne, 216
grapefruit(s):
  in citrus fruit parfait, 55
  pineapple breakfast juice, 51
green beans, *see* haricots verts
guests, 39, 63–64, 110, 130

ham and cheese pie, 27
haricots verts (green beans):
  marinated, with crispy leeks, 114
  in a trio of summer salads with bal-
    samic vinegar, 111
  herbed goat cheese, portobellos with
    balsamic glaze and, 146
  herbs, Provençal, chicken breast with
    truffles and, 148
hot fudge sauce, simple, 197

ice cream, white chocolate, chocolate
  waffles with, 198
Inn at Eastport, 3–4
Inn at Twin Linden:
  kitchen of, 7–8, 48
  renovation of, 7–8, 25–26
  restaurant of, 6–8, 88–89, 119, 138
  seasons at, 36, 54, 98, 155
  selection and purchase of, 4, 6

jam, 70

kiwi, in tropical fruit parfait, 56

ladyfingers, 177
lamb:
  rack of, with mint pesto and chèvre
    crust, 139
  tenderloin with ginger soy glaze, 140
leeks:
  crispy, marinated green beans with, 114
  lobster tarts with dill cream and, 165
lemon:
  mascarpone mousse, frozen, 217
  sabayon with raspberries, 217
  shrimp with pesto, pine nuts and, 160
lettuce, washing of, 109
lobster, 165–68
  basics for, 167
  and Brie custards, oven-puffed, 22
  with fingerling potatoes and citrus
    sauce, 166–67
  fricassee with corn and chive pan-
    cakes, 168
  salad with roasted peaches,
    131

tarts with leeks and dill cream, 165
thyme bisque, 86

madeleines, chocolate chip, 184
mango, in tropical fruit parfait, 56
mascarpone:
  lemon mousse, frozen, 217
  strawberry meringues, 172
  venison medallions with cranberries
    and, 151
meat and game, 135–53
  caramelized duck breast with wild
    mushrooms, 152
  quail with roasted strawberry chutney,
    149
  rabbit tenderloins with pumpkin, wild
    rice, and apricots, 153
  venison medallions with cranberries
    and mascarpone, 151
  see also beef; chicken; lamb; veal
Mediterranean eggs, 38
melon(s):
  ball, sparkling, 49
  perfect, 79
Mennonites, 2, 4, 9–12, 112, 169
meringues, strawberry mascarpone, 172
mint(ed):
  pesto, rack of lamb with chèvre crust
    and, 139
  strawberry salad with balsamic vine-
    gar, 113
mocha chocolate pie, 200
molasses cookies, 174
mousse:
  eggnog, 223
  frozen lemon mascarpone, 217
  pumpkin, and gingersnap parfait, 210
mushrooms:
  morels, egg custard with, 23
  portobellos with herbed goat cheese
    and balsamic glaze, 146
  sautéed, over poached eggs, 34
  shiitake, in risotto and egg casserole,
    40–41
  wild, caramelized duck breast with,
    152

oatmeal chocolate chip cookies, 185
olives, in Mediterranean eggs, 38
omelets:
  with coulis, 34
  roll, wilted spinach and Gorgonzola,
    43
onion(s), sweet:
  and asparagus tart, 32–33
  caramelized, baked eggs with, 35
onion tart, caramelized, beef tenderloin
  with, 136
orange(s), orange juice:
  cantaloupe soup, 78

champagne granita, 216
  in citrus fruit parfait, 55
  crepes with strawberry-rhubarb glaze,
    68–69
  peach breakfast juice, 50
  in sparkling strawberry soup, 80
  in spiced cranberry pear soup, 76
  in strawberry fizz, 48
  in very berry smoothie, 49
oyster and pancetta chowder, 96

palmiers, almond, 179
pancakes:
  apple and walnut, 73
  with berries and mascarpone, baked, 71
  corn and chive, lobster fricassee with,
    168
pancetta:
  and oyster chowder, 96
  in risotto and egg casserole, 40–41
  spinach with shallot-Gorgonzola
    vinaigrette and, 106
  veal chop with ginger, pear and, 145
parfaits:
  fruit, *see* fruit parfaits
  pumpkin mousse and gingersnap, 210
peach(es):
  baked French toast with blueberries
    and, 59
  orange breakfast juice, 50
  pie, cinnamon, 208
  roasted, lobster salad with, 131
  smoothie with blueberry swirl, 51
peanut butter cookies, 188
pear(s):
  in brioche French toast with fall fruit,
    60–61
  and cherry clafouti, 219
  cranberry soup, spiced, 76
  poached, with Stilton and Belgian
    endive, 108
  veal chop with ginger, pancetta and,
    145
pecan(s):
  fudge tart, 202
  shortbread bars, 178
  smoked trout, and potatoes with
    creamy dill dressing, 120
pepper, roasted yellow, soup with garlic
  cream, 90
peppers, red bell, in coulis, 34
pesto:
  basil, salmon with polenta crust and,
    162
  basil, shrimp with lemon, pine nuts
    and, 160
  mint, rack of lamb with chèvre crust
    and, 139
pies, dessert, 209
  apple sour cream, 214